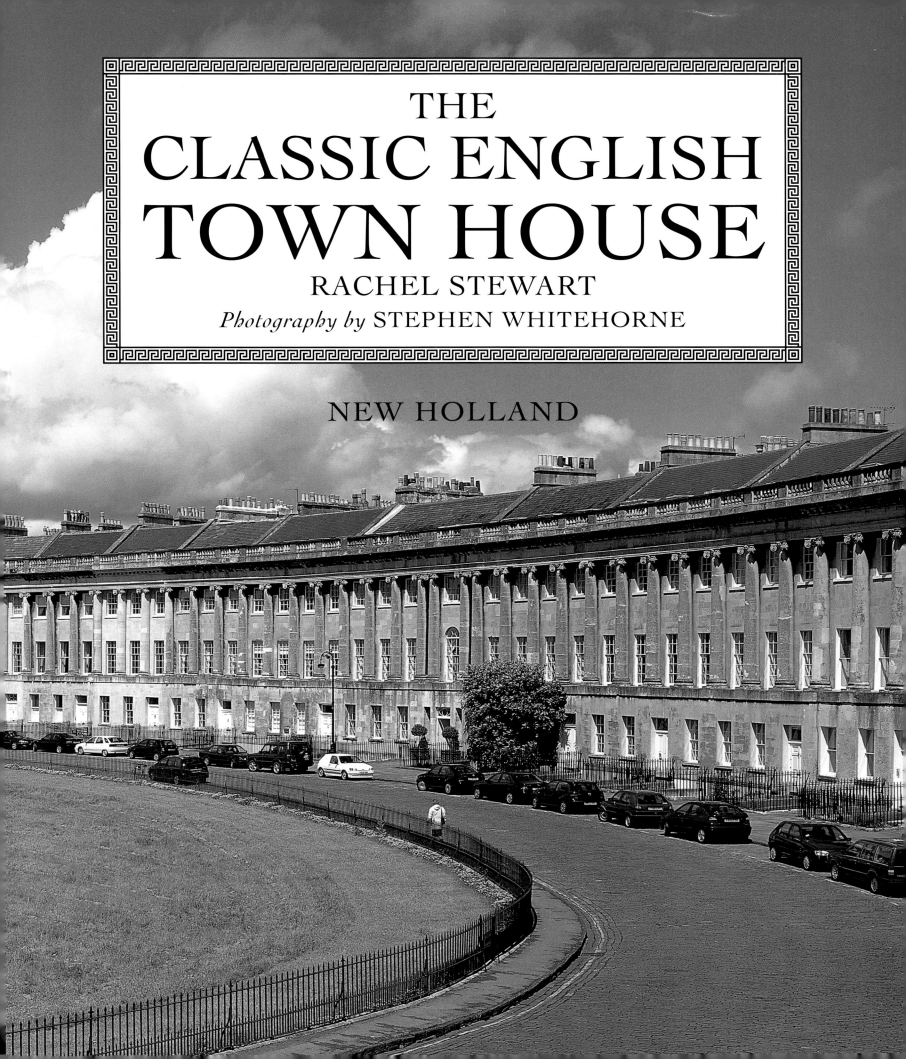

THE
CLASSIC ENGLISH
TOWN HOUSE

RACHEL STEWART

Photography by STEPHEN WHITEHORNE

NEW HOLLAND

First published in 2006 by New Holland Publishers (UK) Ltd
London • Cape Town • Sydney • Auckland

www.newhollandpublishers.com

Garfield House, 86–88 Edgware Road, London, W2 2EA, UK

80 McKenzie Street, Cape Town 8001, South Africa

14 Aquatic Drive, Frenchs Forest, NSW 2086, Australia

218 Lake Road, Northcote, Auckland, New Zealand

10 9 8 7 6 5 4 3 2 1

ISBN 1 84537 115 1

Publishing Manager: Jo Hemmings
Senior Editors: Kate Michell, Julie Delf and Steffanie Brown
Designer: Alan Marshall
Assistant Editor: Kate Parker
Cartographer: Bill Smuts
Production: Joan Woodroffe

Reproduction by Pica Digital Pte Ltd, Singapore
Printed and bound by Kyodo Printing Co Pte Ltd, Singapore

COVER AND PRELIMINARY PAGES

FRONT COVER: Lewis Crescent, Kemp Town, Brighton

SPINE: Entrance hall and staircase at 1 Royal Crescent, Bath

BACK COVER: 18-22 Bedford Square, London

FRONT FLAP: 49, 51 & 53 Pont Street, London

BACK FLAP: The Circus, Bath

HALF-TITLE PAGE: 44 Friar Gate, Derby

TITLE PAGE SPREAD: The Royal Crescent, Bath

OPPOSITE: Bedford Square, London

PAGE 6 (top to bottom): Calverley Park Crescent, Tunbridge Wells; Bay windows at 99 Park Lane, London; 52 Pont Street, London

PAGE 7: Staircase at Handel House, Brook Street, London

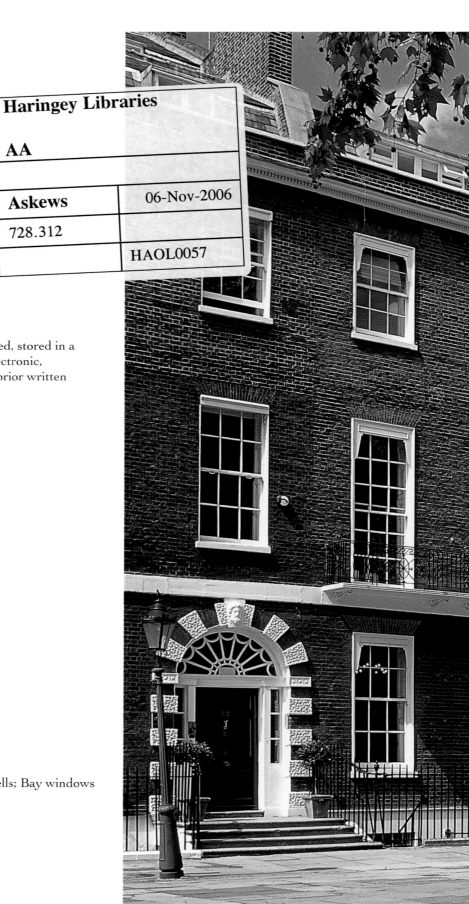

CONTENTS

INTRODUCTION

The term 'town house' can conjure up any one of an array of images, from a smart, detached 18th-century mansion in the town, set within in its own grounds, to a compact 20th-century home on a housing estate with an integral garage. But the most persistent image is that of the smarter Georgian terraced property, which is 'classic' in related senses, being both a seemingly timeless design, repeated over and over in its own era and across the centuries, and also governed in its design by the principles of classical architecture.

OPPOSITE: The tasteful mid-18th-century proportions and décor of the Dining Room at Fairfax House, York.

BELOW: Stylish doorcases smarten up otherwise plain façades to create elegant houses at Rodney Street, Liverpool.

It enjoys the best of both worlds. Like its country counterparts, the Georgian terraced house can be grand and refined, yet, at the same time, its position in a terrace requires it to be sleek, convenient and relatively compact. Its façade, at least, is written in the same classical language as its country cousin, yet the town house need only go so far, and it responds to the imperatives of urban living in its planning,

8

rather than Palladian symmetry. In this paradoxical way, its location in town gives it a certain freedom born of restriction: because it cannot be what the country house is, it is allowed to be something else – it gets to live by its own rules, and excel within them. For this reason, I would argue, the classic English town house is not the grand, detached town mansion set in its own grounds, which responds little to its location in town because it is not required to do so. Rather, it is the five-storey, three- to five-bay house, sharing party walls with its neighbours; expanding upwards rather than outwards; self-contained and self-assured – a private box in the theatre of town.

The Georgian terraced house, in both its grand and more modest manifestations, therefore receives considerable attention in this book. But it is not the lone representative of the English town house. Even where town houses of other periods do not overlap stylistically with the Georgian town house, they still share common elements that contribute to the nature of the English town house itself. We certainly have to admit the Victorian town house to the fold - glorious and 'classic' in its own right, if largely or wholly abandoning the 'classical' in its design principles. The grand 19th-century town house, like the 18th-century house before it, reflected the new conditions of its making. What's more, with classical design principles shrugged off, and both town-house market and town bounds expanding, the Victorian house had scope to make successive changes to its public face to reflect the successive architectural styles of the 19th and early 20th centuries. And neither the 18th- or 19th-century town house can be understood without some knowledge and understanding of its predecessors in earlier centuries.

As well as travelling across the centuries, the town house travelled across the country. While London gets much attention here – justified by its role as a trendsetter, as well as the largest English city by far throughout the period under discussion – the book also examines examples from many other towns and cities, both in relation to the capital but also in their own context. The industrial towns of the north and the spa and seaside resorts of the south followed different paths, even if many of the houses in these locations took the same form. The interplay between these sites and the capital is critical to the story of both.

Little is said about suburbs in this book. The classic English town house is generally not found in suburban areas. When suburbs developed in the later 19th century, suburban architectural styles developed to fit the bill, and their story is another book altogether. Suburban life does not equate with town life, and the

town house was neither suited to nor reflective of the distinctly different, if adjacent, kind of life there. None the less, the classic English town house has cropped up in some surprising places over the years and most recently on out-of-town housing developments.

The English town house has an enduring appeal well beyond that warranted by the convenience of its accommodation and urban situation. While the country house was – and is – tucked away on a remote estate, viewed only with some effort and permission, the town house has always been right there on the street, in the public eye, ready to receive both criticism and admiration. This book carries on a tradition of scrutiny, and looks at change and constancy in the English town house over the years.

ABOVE: The new-build town house revives classic proportions and styling at Poundbury, near Dorchester, Dorset.

OPPOSITE TOP:
Classically styled, stuccoed terraces greet the sea at Lewes Crescent, Kemp Town, Brighton.

OPPOSITE BOTTOM:
Variety in classical styling on wide-fronted town houses at Friar Gate, Derby.

CHAPTER ONE

SHAPING THE FUTURE

The Early Town House

This aim of this book is to trace the development of the town house up to and beyond what I will unashamedly call its pinnacle – the classic Georgian town house. This is not to say that the Georgian house is the 'best'; only that it has been the most enduring, as have certain of its qualities, as we will see when we reach the end of this story. This book is also concerned with a 'classic' form, not just with the story of the town house, hence the heavy bias towards the 18th century. So, without arguing that the classic Georgian town house was inevitable, it is possible to trace its development and account for it. In looking, as we do in this chapter, at the town houses of the medieval period and the 16th and 17th centuries, it is not necessary to be concerned with every twist and turn in the development of the town house, but with those aspects of its development that lead us towards the town house of later centuries, so that we can carry forward those elements that were carried forward, and leave behind those that were discarded.

Jew's House, Lincoln

SPLENDOUR AND SECURITY
The Medieval Town House

It is possible to identify three primary categories of medieval town house. Between them, these three types of house – the aristocratic 'inn', the merchant house and the row house – bear features that can be recognized in later houses. The first two are far removed from the classic town house (within the scope of this book), but each has elements in common with it, or that differ from it in ways that help to explain how the classic model developed.

The Aristocratic Inn

Of these three types of medieval dwelling, the aristocratic house appears to bear the least resemblance to the later models inhabited by the same class, largely because of the very different circumstances in which the nobility lived in the Middle Ages. The medieval lord had an extensive household, which could number as many as 150 individuals, including immediate and more distant family members, servants, advisors and agents. A subsection of this household was his 'riding' or 'foreign' household, which might number 50 people who went with him wherever he went, including to town. In addition to the riding household, a medieval lord also took many of his more costly 'quality' possessions to town, such as soft furnishings, plates and even furniture. Like his later counterparts,

he went to London, or other major cities such as Norwich or York, to transact business, to buy and to sell and to commission and deliver goods. The lord, his household and his property had a peripatetic existence that is hard to imagine now, especially considering the prevailing transport and travel challenges of the time. What of his house in town, then?

From the 13th century the town houses of the wealthiest aristocrats or merchants sprawled greedily over substantial sites. The term 'inn', which was often used to describe the medieval aristocratic town house, conjures up an image of these buildings more adequately than the alternative terms in use, such as 'palace', 'place' or simply 'house'. These dwellings offered extensive accommodation for working, trading, eating, cooking, entertaining and

RIGHT: Sundry buildings grouped around the courtyard at Arundel House, Strand, London. From an etching by Hollar.

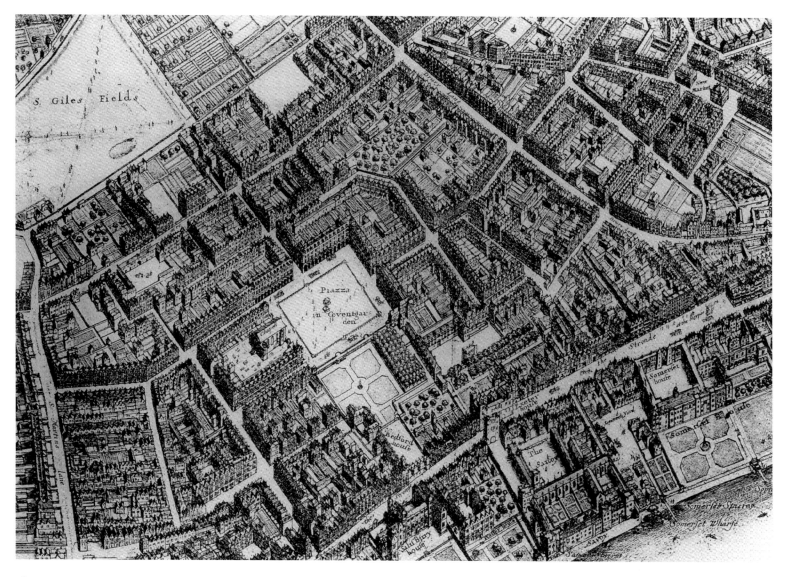

sleeping. Despite the extensive size of many of these sites, a lord's riding household could be so large that some of its members still had to rent lodgings outside the inn.

There was no 'aristocratic quarter' in London, especially in the City proper. Lordly inns were hugger-mugger with the living and working accommodation of merchants, tradesmen and the ubiquitous poor. The inn itself generally turned its back on its neighbours, facing inwards around a courtyard, and shying away behind a screen of taller commercial buildings that bordered the street. These street-facing buildings formed part of the lord's property, but were leased out to turn a profit.

The extensive guest accommodation provided by an inn could be put to commercial use in the lord's absence, as many less wealthy visitors to London were either happy or only able to hire rooms for the duration of a visit rather than incur the great expense of a private inn of their own. Some inns were run as entirely commercial ventures, having been purchased from failing noblemen. And following the dissolution of the monasteries in the 1530s, many aristocratic inns were former ecclesiastical inns that had been acquired by gift or purchase. Some bishops' palaces remained in evidence, particularly those grouped along the Strand in London and still visible on Hollar's map of 1656, although by that time they were in the hands of secular and often commercial owners.

In provincial towns, a lord's inn might

ABOVE: Hollar's map (1656) shows a pattern of courtyard-based medieval inns lining London's Strand, and the recently erected Piazza at Covent Garden.

15

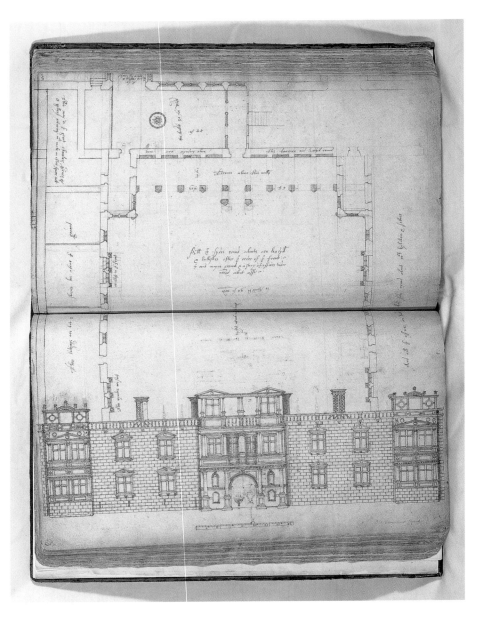

ABOVE: *John Thorpe's drawing of the Strand front to the 16th-century Somerset House, presenting a grand entrance to the courtyard beyond.*

the hall, which was the focus of the complex and usually found on one side of the courtyard. The hall had a high and low end, the latter for more intimate or privileged guests, so there was a certain symbolism inherent in these structures, even from the outside, which was lost in later aristocratic houses. However stately the hall, though, its impact was somewhat mitigated by the other more humble buildings clustered about it.

There is otherwise scant evidence for the form and finish of these houses, and much of what we know comes to us in glimpses from inventories, estate records, diaries and other non-architectural sources. Even London offers little hard evidence for their existence, although it is better represented than most towns and cities in other respects, and therefore dominates this discussion, as it does all writing on the medieval town house. Historian Caroline Barron suggests that the medieval aristocratic house in London may not have been particularly striking, that 'the structure – the architectural style – of the town house did not express the lord's taste or respond very markedly to fashion', and that few were new builds. Inventories from the period suggest that these houses impressed more with their temporary contents than their outward appearance.

Although the aristocratic inn seems far removed in form and façade from the grand street house of later periods, its relationship with its neighbours betrays a factor that will prove very important in subsequent parts of this story. As mentioned earlier, the range of inn buildings fronting the street was often put to good financial use by the inn owner. Shops are best placed on streets and street frontage attracts a premium, so the more plots that could reasonably be fitted in, the more money a landlord could raise through rental. Frontages were typically between 13 and 26 feet (4 and 8 metres) wide, and sufficient area for a burgage, the principal unit of medieval urban land, could only be

form an 'aristocratic quarter' in itself, dominating the town, as at Gainsborough Old Hall, which was begun in 1462 and enhanced with towers in time for a visit from Richard III in 1483. But the inward-looking principle remained, and the inn was a settlement within a settlement, rather than a single monument to aristocratic power, status or taste.

There was often little or no external show, although towers, which were sometimes crenellated under royal licence, might rise to indicate to the outside world that someone grand was secreted beyond the inn gates. The gatehouse itself might also make quite a display. Visitors entering the gates might be impressed by the size of

gained by extending a plot backwards, making it characteristically long and thin. And, in what seems like a counterintuitive way, the narrowest plots were often deemed the best and the wider plots less popular.

It is worth noting that at this early point in city life, the degree of self-sufficiency required of the town dweller was not far off that required of the country dweller, and a lord needed considerable space in and around his inn to provide for his extensive household. As a result, gardens were an important feature of the large house, not only for leisure, but also to provide produce for the household, and perhaps for sale. It was many centuries before the urban became truly urban, shaking off rural touches such as grazing sheep and herds of cattle, which were familiar to the end of the 18th century, even in London.

The development of towns and cities was certainly not a relentless march towards the intense urbanization that was witnessed in the 19th century. In medieval times, the fortunes of towns generally, and some more than others, waxed and waned – often the latter. Urban areas were particularly vulnerable to the Black Death, which wreaked havoc from 1348 and depleted the country's population by a third in its first manifestation. Even boosts to the economy, such as that offered by the Hundred Years' War (1337–1453), were not necessarily centred on towns. As a result, building activity was often static; there was no impetus for urban development, and so none for architectural development. Old houses remained in use for centuries, although doubtless not through any fondness for a 'period property'. In Lincoln, for example, many rather small stone houses, erected by merchants in the 12th century when the city was thriving, survived into the 19th century. Had the city's success been sustained, their

ABOVE: Stone construction, window mouldings, doorcase decoration and a prominent chimneystack mark out the medieval occupant of the Jew's House, Lincoln, as a successful merchant.

ABOVE: *A 16th-century house at Shrewsbury revels in decorative devices in its upper storeys, and makes a splendid show of the type that would scarcely be matched even in the grandest terraces of later days.*

shortcomings in terms of size and lack of flexibility would soon have led to their replacement by larger and more adaptable houses.

Merchant Houses

These stone merchant houses – part of our second medieval type – became known by association as 'Jews' houses'. Their construction was based around the means of raising money and the need to protect it. Out of necessity they were simple buildings, with living quarters raised above a ground floor and a vaulted undercroft given over to storage, manufacture and commercial use. The first floor might contain just two rooms: an upper hall and sleeping accommodation. The Jew's House at Lincoln still stands as an emblem of how status and means could be expressed in a rather modest manner: it is a very simple two-storey building, but its carved entrance and the chimney stack rising above proclaims its status, while its sturdiness and its raised living accommodation above the bustle, threats and smells of the street signify both strength and safety. Lincoln's Jew's House therefore presents a satisfying, relatively broad face to the street, in an otherwise plain building, and says something about the status of its occupant; and these are factors that need to be carried forward to the discussion of the town house in subsequent centuries. In later years, timber-framed medieval houses made equally slight concessions to urban conditions, combining a hall with a chamber above that sat parallel to the street, with a gabled cross-wing end on to it. But at least timber-framed houses were more adaptable than stone examples, as their persistence in modified forms behind later façades attests in many English towns.

The use of stone to build, and especially to ornament buildings as a statement of fashion and status persisted into later periods. Some cities, such as Lincoln, had ready supplies of stone to hand. Other towns, such as Canterbury, expressed status through stone quite against the odds. Cheaper timber and advances in carpentry meant that stone largely gave way to wood in the 13th century – even where there was a good local stone supply in some cases – but stone never lost its cachet. Towards the end of the Middle Ages, the art of brick-making was revived, and brick became a fashionable alternative to stone as a means of aggrandizing buildings. The advantage of timber, however – apart from its price – was that it could, quite literally, be turned to great effect. Wood also offered a new and cheaper means of ornamenting houses. The disadvantage was its flammability, which was demonstrated on a massive scale by the Great Fire of London in 1666, and also by the razing of several other towns in whole or part in the Early Modern period that followed the Middle Ages. From the point of view of this book, however, this flammability was good news for the development of the classic English town house.

Despite the tendency of money to leave town for the country, there were some great and wealthy citizens, including William Canynges the Younger of Bristol and William Grevel of Chipping Camden, who built urban houses that were very much the forerunners of what was to come. Canynges had a splendid house in Redcliffe Street, which demonstrated that a narrow frontage need not indicate meanness, and certainly did not preclude grandeur. It was built in stone and on the grandest of scales, even though it had a frontage of only 28 feet (8.5 metres). What it lacked at the front, it made up for behind, extending to a depth of over 200 feet (60 metres). This provided space for shops or service rooms at the fore and a magnificently finished open hall, 33 feet long and 22 feet wide (10 by 6.7 metres) beyond. The hall formed an elaborate entrance to an ornately tiled family parlour at the rear, beyond which was a tower that overlooked the River Avon.

The Row House

Further down the ranks of medieval dwellings the 'row house' developed. This was the humble predecessor of all terraced town houses, great and small. Such houses responded directly to urban conditions: they were built end-on to the street to form rows, with an internal or external passage leading to the back of the house. Beginning as simply a hall at ground level, with a solar, or chamber, above, this type of dwelling progressed easily to form what would much later be called a 'two-up, two-down'. The hall often moved to the first floor, giving way to commercial premises at the front, with a kitchen or parlour behind. In its elevated position, it ceased to have the ceremonial connotations of a hall proper, but retained a degree of architectural primacy within the house, settling into its new and lasting role as the principal reception room. In addition, there was often a cellar below ground, and second, third and possibly fourth floors and garrets above.

The row house was ubiquitous. It can be distinguished from the later 'terraced house' because each dwelling was conceived and constructed independently. Strictly speaking, terraced houses are

ABOVE: Seventeenth-century fronts loosely mask the halls and cross wings of medieval houses at St Paul's Street, Stamford.

conceived and often built as one unit, which lends each unit a degree of uniformity less evident in individual houses that are simply huddled in a row. There were fewer terraced houses in medieval England, not least because they required a greater investment of planning and money; nevertheless, rows of more-or-less identical houses were certainly built in London from the 14th century onwards.

Both the row house and the terraced house of the medieval period at least recognized that building upwards was the best use of urban space, a practice that suited both builders and occupants, as it would for centuries to come. However, although rural imports often made little sense in town, they persisted against the grain of urban efficiency.

Although it received a town charter in 1332, Smarden, in Kent, was probably never much more than a village, but its exceptional wealth during the medieval period is expressed in several surviving houses. Although magnificent, these houses are rural in character, which poses a question that we must keep in mind on our chronological journey towards the 18th century – when, where, why and how does a town 'aesthetic' begin to emerge? Certainly there was little evidence of its occurrence in the medieval period, when even row houses seem to have responded to town circumstances through necessity rather than 'design', while larger houses and inns simply retained a character that was borrowed from the country.

BELOW: *Rows of houses built and modified at different times still reach across to greet each other at Stonegate, York.*

OLD HABITS AND NEW EXPRESSIONS

The Town House in the Sixteenth and Seventeenth Centuries

A s the medieval period gave way to the Tudor age, three principal types of town house were in evidence. Firstly, there was the inn-type 'house' which, as in the previous era, differed little from its manorial counterparts in the country. As before, these larger houses were often hidden and secluded from the city surrounding them by the taller, meaner commercial buildings rented out along their street fronts.

BELOW: Bay windows increasing in size over three floors, and Renaissance mouldings emphasize the height and individuality of a 16th-century house on the corner of Fleet Street and Chancery Lane, London. A steeply pitched roof completes the work (J. T. Smith, 1789).

This expansive type of courtyard property fairly soon – and somewhat inevitably – gave way to other types of dwelling that were less greedy in their consumption of precious and often costly urban space. Its noble occupants were also increasingly disinclined to risk their health and safety for extended periods in the polluted and plague-ridden urban areas. In a very few cases, this type of house developed into a more formally designed courtyard form, as at Northumberland House on London's Strand. Construction began in 1608 and the house included corner turrets and a marvellously ornate carved frontispiece. Like their predecessors, however, dwellings like Northumberland House were virtually indistinguishable from their rural counterparts. In many respects this particular example resembled the great house at Audley End in Essex, although within the limitations of a town site.

The row house also remained in the Tudor period, essentially with two rooms per floor, one at the front and one at the back. This type of dwelling had the brightest future, even if it gave little impression of this in its earlier days. Its format responded to lack of urban space exactly as the courtyard house did not, hence its

ABOVE: Sixteenth-century Sherar's Mansion, Shrewsbury, creates a house suitable for a wealthy merchant by repeating the row house unit three times over to give an appropriately grand street frontage. Engraving c.1573 after J.C. Buckler in Owen and Blakeway, History of Shrewsbury.

there are few extant houses from the 16th century and even the 17th, especially after the ravages of fires in London and elsewhere, but illustrations from a variety of sources give us some idea of the general appearance of town houses in this period, if not their exact identity. The impression of a relentless series of street-front gable ends is unsurprising, given that larger houses simply replicated the external appearance of smaller houses several times over.

This multiple-fronted house persisted up to the Restoration (1660), and somewhat beyond, although legislation and alternative, classical means of expression eventually saw its demise. Sherar's Mansion itself had hints of styles to come, with Renaissance consoles appearing to support the jetties, but it was essentially Gothic in both construction and style.

Moving Towards a Classic Style

The first evidence of a move towards a classically fronted London town house can be found in records from 1618–19. The houses of Sir Fulke Greville and Lady Cooke in Holborn, as recorded by the architect John Smythson, both featured projecting central bays and a gable with scrolled sides rising to a pediment above a classical cornice. The source for these gables was likely to have been publications by Italian architects and theorists. The segmental gable at Lady Cooke's house may have been inspired by illustrations in *Libro Estraordinario*, which was written by the Italian architect Sebastiano Serlio (1475–1554).

The 'Holborn gable' was popular through the 1630s and 1640s, and spread to the country house too, before giving way in both areas to the hipped roof and eaves cornice. It reappeared in the later 19th century as part of a conscious revival of pre-classical motifs in English architecture. Also evident in Smythson's drawings is the introduction of the cross-window, with a central mullion crossed by a transom a little above its centre – another loosely 'Italian' innovation.

enduring popularity from its medieval birth onwards. However, it was not enough in itself to cater for the needs of Elizabethan England's wealthy merchants – it was not big enough and it did not look impressive enough. The answer, for those that wanted more, was to multiply the row, or unit, house so that the Tudor town witnessed the development of a third main house type: the double-fronted, triple-fronted or even quadruple-fronted house with a row of gables on the street front, as was seen at Sherar's Mansion, Shrewsbury, a building that was completed sometime before 1573. This splendid timber-framed house had three storeys, with the top storey of each of its three parts rising into a gable. The upper storeys were 'jettied', so that they protruded into the street, and all floors had shallow bay windows, the broadest on the first and second floors. It was essentially a row or unit house multiplied by three – and as one house could look like a row, later a row would be made to look like one house (see page 60). As with the medieval period,

the Front of Bathe House: S.ʳ foulke Gryuell: in houlborn 1619

Together, the hipped roof, eaves cornice and 'cross-window' marked a definitive move from medieval building to a new architecture that was decorated with classical forms, even if it did not fully articulate them.

But the path of history never runs true, and while such experimental classicizing was occurring in Holborn, something at once more retrograde and splendid was afoot elsewhere in London. The bays at Sherar's Mansion and the houses of Lady Cooke and Sir Fulke Greville may seem ornate to those of us who are accustomed

to restrained classicism in town-house fronts, but the decoration here was nothing compared to that which adorned some of the most splendid houses of the early 17th century. Of these, the best-known in London is the house, or at least house front, of Sir Paul Pindar, a major figure in the realms of Jacobean trade and diplomacy. Returning from a successful and financially enriching career in the Levant, Sir Paul settled in Bishopsgate in 1624. The magnificently and ornately carved timber front of his house, which thankfully survived the Great Fire, is now in the

ABOVE: Sir Fulke Greville's house at Holborn, London, recorded in 1619, combines loosely classical motifs with a distinctive Holborn gable.

23

gable. A gallery above the gables diminished the external effect of their role still further. And, in conjunction with the multiple house front, such galleries counteracted the vertical emphasis of the building, and hinted a little at the horizontal influence that would govern rows of town houses so emphatically a century later.

The Tudor and Stuart monarchs were keen on building legislation, although much of it was concerned more with controlling London's growth than dictating and enforcing building standards. But in 1605, James I (1566–1625) banned the use of timber fronts on new houses, partly for the practical reasons of conserving timber supplies and as some protection against fire, but also to encourage a degree of uniformity. The decree demanded that all outer walls were to be made of brick or stone. This legislation was bolstered by a quick succession of further proclamations, including, in 1611, measures against the construction of jetties over 18 inches (45 centimetres) as well as timber building generally. In 1615 James declared his intention to be remembered as a monarch who had found the 'City and suburbs of stickes, and left them of Bricke'. Certainly, he perceived that the overall appearance of London's domestic architecture would reflect well or ill on the city and the country, and therefore on the king himself. Brick was more durable, fireproof, 'beautiful and magnificent'. Successive proclamations dictated brick sizes, storey heights and, more loosely, relative window dimensions, taking an important first step towards uniformity in new buildings. Jetties and projecting windows were outlawed and walls were to 'goe direct and strait upwards'. Some elements of this legislation may reflect the influence of the King's Surveyor-General and member of the Buildings Commission, Inigo Jones, of whom more later (see pages 25-27).

However, this legislation had limited application, as it was often only concerned with the City of London proper and perhaps a short distance beyond. It was also

Victoria & Albert Museum. It is ornate in every aspect: in the treatment of the myriad of small panes of glass, in its carved panels and even in its profile. The impact of the bays at Pindar's house and elsewhere was to take away much of the responsibility for street effect from the

concerned more with matters of licensing than the strict prohibition of new building, and was often ignored in any case. Beyond the City of London, in the absence of legislative control, timber building remained the rule. Brick and stone town houses of this period tended to be, as the noted architect and author John Summerson (1904–1992) stated, 'exceptionally large and for exceptional people', and, as before, offered accommodation of a scale and format that was comparable with a country house. Otherwise, timber-built merchant houses four or five storeys high leaned out over streets in towns such as Exeter and Bristol well into the second half of the 17th century, with little regard for significant new movements that were taking place in the capital.

Covent Garden

Legislation sometimes took unexpected forms. In 1630 Charles I (1600–49) gave permission for the Earl of Bedford to develop his estate at Covent Garden on the condition that the earl employed the king's own architect. In effect, this was a form of design legislation, as this position was occupied by England's first 'classical' architect, Inigo Jones (1573–1652). The resulting development, only parts of which now remain, plays a significant part in this story for two reasons. First, the original piazza at Covent Garden brought to the secular domestic arena the type of uniformity and overarching design previously reserved for groups of dwellings in collegiate or ecclesiastical environments. The king's edict, as well as the extent of Bedford's finances and land holdings, both dictated and permitted a degree of uniformity that more piecemeal developments and redevelopments could not hope to display. As ever, builders and developers were unlikely to choose to subordinate their personal ends and means to the greater end of uniformity or at least visual cohesiveness – unlike a lord with land and money to play with and his king's beady eye fixed on him.

Second, the piazza included influences that were clearly Continental, most notably Italian. These features were evident in both the basically symmetrical urban square with its regular façades and also in the design of the façades themselves. The latter resemble the elevation for a courtyard façade at the urban Palazzo Thiene in Vicenza (1540s), as illustrated in *Quattro Libri dell'Architettura* (1570) by the celebrated Renaissance architect Andrea Palladio (1508–1580), and a design for a town house from Sebastiano Serlio's *Seventh Book of Architecture*. Palladio and Serlio's publications were frequently treated in the manner of pattern-books by 17th- and 18th-century architects searching for leads and ideas in their attempts to let some brand of classicism loose on the English public. However, none were as assiduous as Jones in closely observing, understanding and annotating Palladio's designs. In addition to the palazzi of the Italian Renaissance, Covent Garden piazza could count among its forebears the Place Royale (now the Place des Vosges) in Paris. Its appearance was only novel in an

ABOVE: *Inigo Jones's uniform classical façades at Covent Garden, London, eschew all home-bred Artisan Mannerism and offer the first clues of what was to replace it on the urban scene. The bustling commercial activity in the centre is at odds with the well-managed landscaping of the 18th-century residential square.* Covent Garden Piazza and Market, *John Collet, c.1775.*

English context, not in a Continental sense. As a result, English architecture of this period is often presented as somehow backward: it either ignores or misunderstands Continental classicism or it catches up with it in good style but a little late in the day. In such narratives, Inigo Jones saves us from ourselves, showing us that stirring a few disembodied elements of classicism into our melting pot of decorative motifs and slapping them on the front of our buildings merely betrays our ignorance of how things should be done 'properly'. The Georgian town house is often portrayed as the butterfly bursting beautifully and perfectly out of the chrysalis of ignorant, ugly and incorrect 'Artisan Mannerism', the term used somewhat disparagingly to describe a less-than-educated approach to the elements of classicism. But these earlier buildings fulfilled the desires of their builders – they were not

failed attempts at creating a classical town-house façade. They have to be appreciated for their own merits rather than sneered at for not achieving an ideal defined in a different time and place.

In any case, Covent Garden seems to have been shuffled into the wrong place in the history of English urban domestic architecture, and it offers a sharp lesson to anyone inclined to see history as an inevitable and onward-marching progression towards improvement and modernity. Although it set a precedent widely imitated in its essence, if not in its details, this imitation was not significantly manifested until the following century, a delay of nearly one hundred years. For all that its principal influences derived from distant times and places, Covent Garden was modern in its context. But it did not mark an architectural watershed, even in London. With hindsight it can be viewed as a sign of what was to come, and we wait rather impatiently for its promise to be fulfilled, but it is unlikely that the men and women of 17th-century London spotted a classic in the making. If a play of *c.*1632 is anything to go by, what they did recognize, and liked, was how the surveyor had 'wedded strength to beauty; state to uniformity; commodiousness with perspicacity! All, all as't should be!'

The idea of regularized façades did catch on, as did the greater or lesser use of classical proportions and ornament. As we will see, the rusticated ground floor forming a pedestal or podium that leads to a real or implied 'giant order' of pilasters bracing the two storeys above becomes part of the town house 'aesthetic' (see Chapter Two, pages 56-62). At Covent Garden, in a not very Italianate manner, dormer windows serve a further storey in the undisguised attic. Later manifestations of the classical town house often attempted to mask the traditional – and advisable – English sloping roof behind a screen or balustrade, giving the impression of a flat head to the building and a more faithfully classical appearance.

It is not possible to determine that all future classicizing touches on town houses derived from Jones's example at Covent Garden. Such influences are both varied and hard to pin down, as we will later see. It is difficult enough to trace sources and influences with any certainty when dealing with 'high' architecture – for example, the architect-designed and well-documented country house. It is harder still to pinpoint influences when much of the practice with which we are concerned eventually became repetitive and virtually habitual and was also exercised by unknown or unexceptional journeymen designer-builders.

Even in the 18th century few develop-

ments replicated Jones's very Italian palazzo-like arcaded ground floor. At Covent Garden it was used to good and appropriate effect as a kind of commercial base for the house, again following the Italian precedent, but demand for this type of dual function fell as the 17th century wore on, and it was even less popular in the 18th century, as the well-to-do were more inclined to keep business and domestic accommodation separate. In fact, flats, not houses, could be found behind the façades of Covent Garden – a surprisingly modern style of living. But this set-up did not catch on, even though, more often than not in the less salubrious parts of town, London's inhabitants tended to live in part rather than all of a house.

One of the reasons that there was a

ABOVE: William Hogarth's image of Covent Garden in the morning, from the 'Times of Day' series, shows a range of loosely classical buildings at the church end of the piazza, and makes clear the area's demise as a fashionable location by the 1730s.

OPPOSITE: *A rusticated ground floor and elegant Ionic columns provide a refined classical front to Lindsey House, Lincoln's Inn Fields, London, one of the first of the kind.*

BELOW: *Houses at Great Queen Street, London, shown in a 1637 engraving, follow Covent Garden's lead in articulating a façade with the help of 'giant' pilasters differentiating the main upper storeys from the ground-floor base. Only the mouldings between first- and second-floor windows betray the early 17th-century date. The format for the classic urban house is now set.*

delay in following the lead that the design of Covent Garden presented was that such developments required knowledge of the classical language of architecture – the architectural equivalent of Latin, we might say. The essential design elements manifested in the project simply weren't at the disposal of every architect. These rules needed to be simplified and codified before they could fall into common usage, and the time was not yet right.

However, the fashion for 'giant' pilasters running the height of two storeys did spread to other London houses, sometimes combined obstinately and awkwardly with Jacobean features such as gables and bay windows, but nevertheless indicating a 'fashionable' progression. Streets that developed in the 1630s, such as Henrietta Street (1630–33) and King Street (1631–37), comprised brick houses that combined individual gable design and a balcony over the door with a trim of pilasters. The new 'classical' features were therefore often combined with an element of personalization that distinguished one house from another, which was at odds

with the more forceful classical design and homogenization of town houses in the early part of the 18th century. But the pilastered house was by no means common in town. Summerson suggests that both owners and speculative developers disliked the emphasis that the 'classical' façade gave to the first floor and its windows, preferring to stick with equal window heights in each storey, something that may have been so. But it is surely as likely that the cost of decorating a house in this way was a deterrent to both parties.

In any case, 'Artisan Mannerist' houses – with shaped gables, quoining, architraved window surrounds, decorative window heads and a selective application of classical elements – coexisted with more regularly classical buildings. Although little architecture remains from this period, it is evident that no simple characterization of urban domestic building styles was apparent in the first half of the 17th century. There were some very notable developments, especially for the purposes of the town house, which came shortly after the construction of Covent Garden and cer-

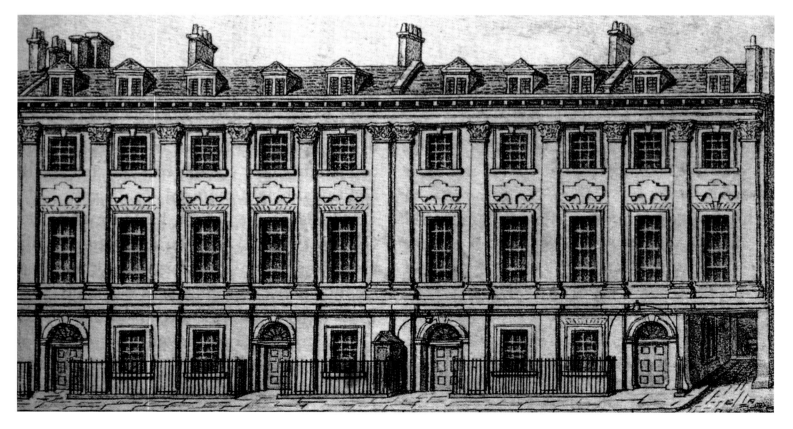

tainly owe more to its classical architecture and uniformity and its precocious presentation of a residential square. In 1636 William Newton obtained a licence to erect 14 houses on his land at Great Queen Street. Each was a substantial 40 feet (12 metres) wide, and they were grouped in a long row within an undeniably formal classical design. These houses, since demolished, had regular windows that were separated by Corinthian pilasters rising over two storeys to an eaves cornice, with the ground floor again acting as a kind of podium for the first and second floors. The paired pilasters at the centre of the group were not 'correct', but in their general form, these buildings were the first true expression of the classic English town house – far more so than Inigo Jones's buildings at Covent Garden. Shortly afterwards, Newton undertook a more ambitious project at Lincoln's Inn Fields, intending to erect a symmetrical composition that comprised a large central house, two slightly lower houses on either side, and still lower houses beyond. Practicalities got in the way of symmetry, but the resulting houses nevertheless had Ionic pilasters, which included playful roses and fleur-de-lis below the capitals.

These columns rose above a rusticated basement, with those of the centre house raised on short pedestals to provide extra height. Now known as Lindsey House, this is the sole survivor of these two developments and as such, Summerson says, 'the most important single house in London'. These are most definitely 'terraced houses', not simply 'row houses', and they are most definitely classical. Once bays and other projecting decorative devices were omitted from buildings, the classical 'order' with pedestals, columns or pilasters and entablature took to its new home on the townhouse front naturally, with little or no compromise on either side. And it served well in taking on the decorative and aggrandizing role of those devices it had ousted.

ABOVE: *Sparrowe's House, Ipswich, depicted here in 1845, belies the assumption that external moderation is always the Englishman's natural preference. Such fronts may not have been abundant, but they show what could be done where legislation did not get in the way of money, ambition and talented craftsmen.*

Sparrowe's House

The provinces were often some way behind London fashions, partly, no doubt, because they were not usually governed by the same restrictive building regulations, particularly in regard to flammable materials, but also because they often had their own regional methods of doing things. In the mid–17th century, several years after the classical innovations in brick and stone at Covent Garden, Great Queen Street and elsewhere, an Ipswich merchant and shopkeeper named Robert Sparrowe extended his house to feature one of the most remarkable extant examples of urban Mannerism. Its idiosyncratic and splendid elaboration represents the pinnacle of intricate timber house fronts, before individuality and flammability and regional variation gave way to a more restrained, economic and fire-resistant building style in brick. It is buildings of this decorative quality that stop us in our tracks on the search for the classic English town house. Sparrowe's house stands for what might have been – and presents a very tempting alternative – although the sheer expense involved in its design and construction would have restricted such design to a few houses in any town. It is worth noting, too, that – just as in the medieval period – the street front was a merchant's best advertisement, so that in towns such as Ipswich, the timbered fronts of commercial premises were more elaborate than the neighbouring brick houses of the clergy and gentry. Sparrowe's House is the antithesis of the severe spirit of the Puritan age, as expressed in bulk in the brick houses of

London and in individual houses in the provinces. It has been described as fusing 'classical detail and vernacular form into an urban ideal', giving a level of 'movement and visual diversity' that was scarcely seen on individual town houses again. The front of Sparrowe's House is truly a composition. It is not a muddled mess or a chance happening – it is a carpenter's approach to classicism. And here classicism is not yet read as synonymous with regularity and restraint and an end in itself, but is a vehicle for an unstinting display of the carpenter's skill and his patron's wealth.

Restoration Residences

Sparrowe's House can be interpreted as something of a culmination and a throwback. Elsewhere, especially in London, the typical house of the Restoration period, which followed shortly after the renovation of Sparrowe's Ipswich house, was very different. It had regular windows that were pretty much the same height on every floor, and its external ornaments were generally limited to key blocks on the windows, bands at the principal floor levels, a modillion eaves cornice, and a loosely classical wooden door case. In plan, the late-17th century house was moving towards the formula that would dominate construction in the following century and beyond: one room at the front and back on each floor, with a staircase at the side and a closet that usually projected at one side to the house's rear. Larger houses were much the same in their details, but spread over five or seven bays, rather than the more usual three. The central portion might have been emphasized by a pediment or by a slight projection forward that was perhaps in turn emphasized visually by stone quoins, giving the house something of the look of contemporary country-house architecture.

The Interregnum (1649–1660), during which the amendments to Sparrowe's house had been undertaken, had brought most building activity to a snail's pace, if

not a halt. With the Restoration, frustrated schemes stood some chance of being realized – if the permission of the Crown could be gained. The revival of the Court brought many noblemen and members of the gentry back to London, exacerbating the existing shortage of upper class housing, although plans were soon afoot to cater for them. Before the Civil War (1642–49), the Earl of Southampton had wished to develop some of his town land, submitting a nondescript scheme for approval that had no merit in terms of ornamenting the city – certainly no pilasters along the lines of those seen at Great Queen Street or Covent Garden. For this and other reasons – such as a recent clash with the Crown – no building licence was granted. However, Southampton kept his scheme in mind

ABOVE: 40 High Street, Exeter, pulls itself away from its neighbours with quoined edges appearing to force the windows together and push out a central projecting bay. The artisan mannerist is at work here, leaving his traces in the brick decoration and the bulky segmental pediment on the second floor.

ABOVE: Cupola House, Bury St Edmonds. Built for a wealthy apothecary in 1693, the house illustrates features fashionable in the late 17th century: narrow windows, contrasting quoins, carved brackets and a cupola.

ABOVE RIGHT: At the back of the spacious town house at Gotham House, Hammets Square, Tiverton, are pilasters and a door and window combination worthy of a front, with linear Y tracery played off against sturdier surrounds.

during the Interregnum, building himself a house on what would later be the north side of Bloomsbury Square, and pegging out the site for terraces on the other sides. With the stylistically unadventurous Sir John Denham (1615–69) in place as Surveyor of the King's Works following the Restoration, a building licence was soon granted and the first leases signed in 1661. The earl handed control to his lessees, who erected 14 regular and distinctly plain houses on each side of the square.

Although the writer John Evelyn referred to the development as a 'Piazza', it had virtually nothing in common with Jones's Covent Garden beyond its general adherence to classical proportions, which

were implemented for the sake of regularity if nothing more. Horizontal bands at the levels of the main floors were the only ornamentation; there were still no pilasters in place or classical ornament. The houses were uniform in front and mean behind, where they faced a purpose-built mews and market, ensuring that the new square was a self-supporting unit as planned. The significance of this development is that, despite – or perhaps because of – its cheapness and blandness, its houses set the pattern for London's residential development over the next 200 years. The square relied for effect on the presence of Southampton House combined with the cumulative effect of three rows of uniform houses, facing each other across a residential square.

It certainly did not rely on the architectural presence of the individual houses.

Following the failure of a more ambitious scheme for individual mansions, St James's Square – consistently one of London's most prestigious locations – followed in much the same pattern. Perhaps in reaction to its initial undistinguished appearance, the site became a hotbed of architectural experiment a hundred years later (see pages 61-62), but at its inception, like much building of the Restoration and after the Great Fire, it scarcely counted as architecture at all. Instead, like Bloomsbury Square, it was a monument to compromise, in which the diverse parties involved in the project – the landlord, the developer, the builder,

the lessees and the craftsmen – settled at a point at which none took any real risks and all were likely to gain. This pattern of construction was set for some considerable time to come.

Beyond the capital, houses in provincial towns often displayed more width and woodwork, indicating more in common with their country counterparts. And just because so much new building was being undertaken in London, we should not forget that much building work in the provinces was concerned with 'modernizing' existing housing stock. Many a medieval house still lay behind a Tudor or Stuart façade, just as many earlier houses would soon wear a Georgian mask in public.

ABOVE: The Red House, Sevenoaks, represents the late 17th-century ideal in a broad town house. It has seven bays, with lower one-bay wings set back at the sides. The main storeys are equal in height. Note the narrower windows at either end, showing a regard for balance rather than uniformity. The large hipped roof has a deep cornice supported on richly carved brackets. The doorcase is a clumsy insertion of the late 18th century.

LAW AND ORDER
The Impact of the Great Fire

Back in London there was no change in the capital's domestic architecture on the scale of the Great Fire. The post-fire rebuilding did not introduce a new building type or style. We simply see what was happening before, but to a greater extent, as the existing unpretentious and financially undemanding prevalent house type lent itself well to the need for speedy rebuilding. The brick terrace did not develop in response to London's Great Fire; it was there already. Even legislation put in place after the event simply formalized what was already beginning to happen, and made it more likely that it did. As architectural historian Elizabeth McKellar observes, the main impact of the legislation was 'to provide a template for the new house which established its frame, dimensions and general typology. Although it was seemingly stylistically neutral, in effect it dictated the new urban vocabulary of uniformity, regularity and minimalism.'

So there was no abrupt change in the style of housing. Construction techniques did not take a big leap in the new, post-fire world, and for some time houses remained essentially timber-framed behind brick façades. There was just more brick than there had been. As late as 1683 the mathematician Joseph Moxon (1627–1700) illustrated a house type in his *Mechanick Exercises* that had certainly persisted into the later part of the 17th century, featuring a gable roof and a very prominent chimney. There is evidence that similar houses were being built with pilasters, just as they had been 60 or so years earlier. Instead, the Great Fire presented an unprecedented opportunity to make the majority of housing stock answerable to prevailing and new building regulations, given that new-built houses would greatly outnumber older homes for the first time. So, if legislation had *tried* to play its part in London before the fire, it had more of an opportunity to run the show after the event. However, the legislation was not prescriptive in terms of how individual houses should look, just how they should be. The 1667 Act for Rebuilding the City classified houses into four types, laying down thicknesses for brick walls and scantlings for timber. Importantly, it also governed the width of streets and the height of buildings, taking an unprecedented holistic approach to town planning and its resultant appearance. The 1667 Act was clearly a major force in the form that London and the town house would take from the later 17th century. But there was another force at work – one that was possibly more powerful. I have already mentioned speculative developers in passing (see pages 32-33), but it was in the post-fire period that this approach to the provision of urban housing at almost all levels came into its own in London. It is, ultimately, the easy combination of speculative development and restrained, urban classicism – the former cheaply and easily turning out the latter – that accounts for the development of the classic English town house. In either case, as I have said, the post-fire legislation simply formalized

what was already being practised at Bloomsbury Square, St James's Square and elsewhere. Even Covent Garden had originally been planned as astylar, and therefore much more restrained than it turned out to be, and it was only changed in response to the intervention of Charles I, hence the giant order of pilasters. House builders simply continued as before, but with more alacrity. 'Denham dullness' was just what was needed for speedy building by developers more concerned with profits than with style, let alone innovation.

The impact of the Great Fire was felt well beyond the City proper. Not only did the capital dictate architectural style to the provinces, but legislation applicable to London and Westminster was often taken as 'best practice' by other civic authorities, or simply as a guide by builders. What is more, several other towns were devastated by fire in the 17th and 18th centuries, and these places no doubt looked to London to lead them in the urgent task of rebuilding, with one eye no doubt fixed on future fire-resistance.

ABOVE: London had experienced many fires before the Great Fire of 1666, some of them called 'great' in their own time, but nothing on this scale. Estimates suggest that around 13,000 houses were destroyed, leaving up to 80,000 Londoners homeless. Etching by Jan Luyken, 1649-1712.

35

CONCLUSION
Restoration and Beyond

Town houses from the Restoration to the early 18th century bridge the gap between the vernacular, regional and personal idiosyncrasies of early times and the omnipresent, levelling high or low classicism of later ones. That does not mean that they should not be taken seriously in their own right. Even within the terms of this particular story, they are more than simple precursors to the 'classic' 18th-century house. There is, in fact, no neat developmental path to be traced, either from the vernacular to the classical, or within the classical itself. The houses of this period are difficult to categorize, and this is what makes them both interesting and also vulnerable to dismissal as being somewhat half-baked.

What points to the past? Well, brick houses were still evolving from previous forms to suit the constraints of the linear plan of the terrace. For example, the position of the staircase supported by the chimneystack at the centre of the house shifted to the rear, where it received light more easily, while the chimneystack moved over to the party wall. It was a sensible response to the new conditions, but it was a process of evolution rather than revolution.

More significantly, individualistic carving remained a feature of houses in both the City and the West End, even into the earlier part of the 18th century. Houses at Queen Anne's Gate (c. 1704) show how some idiosyncrasy and individuality could still be expressed within a fairly standard theme. Strictly speaking, these houses belong in the next chapter, but they demonstrate something that soon disappeared in the 18th century: in addition to a prominent wooden eaves cornice, they have carved keystones above the windows and elaborately carved wooden canopies above the doors. They rely for their effect not on satisfying compositional proportion, as Georgian houses would, but on their compositional detail and elaborate ornamentation. In the City, houses in Laurence Pountney Hill (1703) have exuberant, shell-like hoods, illustrating again something that, while delightful, needed to be sacrificed for the sake of the Palladian classic style that developed soon after.

And what points to the future? The demand for building had existed before the 1666, but it was now worse — or better, depending on your perspective. At the same time, and perhaps for that reason,

BELOW: *Houses at Queen Anne's Gate, London, illustrate the last gasps of individualistic wooden detail articulating and ornamenting the façades of London houses.*

the building industry became more akin to a modern commercial industry, distinct from the local craft industry that had previously prevailed. Although mass production did not take a mechanized form, the repeated use of regular patterns and parts in speculative houses becomes evident; for example, door cases and windows could be brought to the site ready made. It was not so much that there were overall standardized designs, but that each developer or his carpenter had a design that he used repeatedly in his houses. Variety was therefore introduced by different builders developing neighbouring groups of properties, rather than between individual houses, a practice that stopped houses in groups looking the same. Only where one builder, such as the infamous Nicholas Barbon, was responsible for an extensive development did the monotony of standardization become more obvious.

Despite the persistence of elaborate door hoods in some parts, there was less and less scope for carvers on the London house front. A projecting wooden ornament was a fire hazard, and fir was substituted for oak as it lent itself more to 'regularized, cut shapes' rather than ornate freehand carving. Patterns that could be easily repeated were more likely to be lifted from books. Equally, there was little role for the stonemason, as the expense of providing and working stone did not sit well with the economies of speculative building.

Classicism gradually stopped being the province of the knowledgeable, well placed and wealthy, and became the default style for virtually all but the poorest classes. As Elizabeth McKellar writes, classicism's 'essentially geometric forms could be used for both short- and long-run production with variations of detail and scale being possible within the overall frame. From the aristocratic enclave of St James's Square, to the smallest first-rate house in a back alley of the City, to a grand mansion on the outskirts of town, the same basic features were adopted.'

In this period a decline in the popularity of large, urban aristocratic mansions is already evident, as is their conversion to streets of much smaller terraced houses, as at Essex House in the mid-1670s. There was more of this to come in the 18th century, with even terrace-based mansions subdivided into smaller units. Also evident, in writing if not in practice, is a measure of concern about the pace at which London's fields were being covered by new houses. The change was seen, quite rightly, as frightening and irrevocable. At the same time, there was much disappointment that the form that this rapid growth took represented a missed opportunity. Like it or not, we are so used to looking to this period for the roots of the orderly classicism of the 18th century that we overlook the fact that there was much criticism of the way the rebuilding of London fell short of ideals. It was far from being as orderly, convenient or beautiful as it might have been, and the quality of its construction was often pitiful. The 'standard' house of the late 17th and early 18th centuries suited the new consumer society, which burgeoned in the Georgian era. Its basic shell of brick and wood was a characterless box that could

ABOVE: Carved door brackets at No 12 Barn Hill, Stamford, show the kind of impressive woodwork which was soon to disappear in London in the face of fashion and legislation.

ABOVE: *Freely carved and delightful shell canopies at Laurence Pountney Hill, London.*

easily be personalized, upgraded or updated by the addition or replacement of ornament to its exterior, or particularly its interior. As is the case today, an element of choice was often available to purchasers of new properties, especially with regard to interiors, and the market catered for the continual renewal and replacement of these elements.

Although it is possible to identify several different sorts of urban house, and many variants within types, there was still a tendency towards some level of standardization of design – some move towards sameness and away from difference. How was this achieved? Verbal communication certainly remained important in this period, more so than the written word. Most town houses did not feature columns, so the dos and don'ts of handling the classical orders, as contained in architectural treatises, were not especially relevant to the builder. Pattern-books were also of limited value, making very little reference to town

houses. However, books that dealt with subjects such as surveying and measuring must have played a part in standardizing and improving the processes by which buildings were 'designed', even if they had no direct impact on the designs themselves. Unlike some of their successors in the 18th and 19th centuries, they do not prescribe how buildings should look, either in terms of general style or specific features. In this way they worked with the increased standardization of parts and materials to create a kind of core similarity, which happened by default. It seems most likely, however, that design was often a process of following precedent. Many building contracts specified that the houses to be erected had to be constructed in the manner of named houses that had already been built. In effect this was a form of building 'Darwinism', in which selected and existing houses became the pattern for houses yet to be designed.

As far as the 'classical' is concerned, the 17th-century town house borrowed from the classical vocabulary 'only a notion of regularity and some, but by no means all, of its detailing'. It is easy for us to think that this was not doing it 'properly', as it had not quite become what the 18th-century house would be. But the essence of the classic English town house is here. The relative proportions were lacking, but it had the neatness and order and it had the restraint. By the end of the 17th century, the English town house had an essential elegance, even if it could not lay claim to the aesthetic perfection by which we will be struck – without even recognizing what has hit us – in the 'correctly' classical house of the next century. Disregarding the offset door, the 17th century house had a symmetrical brick front, behind which were two main rooms per floor. Decorative elements boiled down to a few essentials. There was little wooden ornament – perhaps a basic eaves cornice and a panelled door with surround. Brick or stone ornament was limited to string courses marking floor levels, and some

play with window heads and keystones.

But before we leave the 17th century, and those elements of its domestic urban architecture that persisted into the century that followed, we might care to stop and think about what we are leaving behind – essentially, just what was sacrificed in the name of what would become the 'classic' English town house. Floor and window heights with little if any distinction between them offer an aesthetic satisfaction of their own. So does the verticality that the combination of relatively narrow windows and piers creates, sometimes emphasized still further by aprons, keystones and other devices that link top to bottom in the individual house and counteract the horizontal effect created by the row itself. We will miss elaborately and idiosyncratically carved door hoods, which are absolutely counter to the aesthetic of 'flatness' that is about to prevail, but are delightful in and of themselves.

However much we admire the town house at its classical 'peak', the fact that such features were discarded was a high price to pay. Looking further back, variant gables will now disappear until the 'classic' period is over. In fact, much of what we miss from these earlier periods – their most interesting, or simply entertaining features – become evident again in the 19th century, in modified forms. Fronts like that to Sparrowe's House disappeared, but they inspired later architects such as Richard Norman Shaw (1831–1913) to produce something equally counter to the classic town house. The celebration of such elaborate forms in the later 1800s marked an abrupt break from the domination of the classic English town house – even more so than the step we are about to take towards it. If it were not for the persistent appeal of the Georgian town house, it would be easy to see it less as an architectural pinnacle and more as an aberration, getting in the way of the more definitively 'English' town houses that preceded and followed it.

ABOVE: Window variety, assorted projections and splendid gables at Pont Street, London, hark back to English urban architecture of the 16th and 17th centuries.

39

CHAPTER TWO

A CLASSIC DEVELOPS

The Town House in the Eighteenth Century

The 18th century is percieved as the glory age of the English town house. But why is this? And was this peak recognized at the time? At the beginning of the century, the house had settled into a general form that provided the basis for what was to follow in abundance, yet it was not a 'classic' at this point. It was the coincidence of the 'rage of building' that occurred in the early decades of the 18th century – most notably in London's West End, and also in Bath – and the rise of Palladianism in Britain that allowed what we now view as the classic English town house to develop. Palladianism promoted and justified a formula for aesthetic success that could be applied again and again to the architecture of the town-house façade. As a result, proportions were tweaked and codified, providing a template for hurried, profit-hungry builders happy to conform to a basic standard that was visually appealing and cost-effective. It also provided a basis for more imaginative designers, who later took the Palladian style as the starting point for stylish and 'classic' treatments of individual houses and terraces.

Nos 18-22 Bedford Square, London

ALL THE RAGE

The Town House in Great Demand and Supply

As in previous periods, there were three principal types of town house in the 18th century. The first type was the freestanding mansion set in its own grounds. Houses like these became increasingly rare, especially in London, as the century progressed, with only around 16 built in the capital in the second half of the century. The next type was the broad-fronted town house, wider than it was deep and set against its neighbours, or very close to them. This type of house was principally confined to provincial towns, where there was likely to be more space, and where the size of the dwelling might reflect the civic status of its owner. Last but by no means least was the terraced house, like its predecessors, far deeper than it was wide and built in its thousands across the country, in towns large and small.

RIGHT: 61 Green Street, London, by architect Roger Morris for himself, displays all the regularity and dullness of the early 18th-century house. Mouldings are minimal, and vertical emphasis is lost. Instead, a strong band at first-floor sill level reaches out to neighbouring houses. Adherence to Palladian proportions and principles here includes a central doorway, but most architects and builders sacrificed such principles for practicality and put their doors to one side.

The terraced house was the main representative of the 18th century's two major urban domestic building booms: the first in the 1720s and 1730s and the second in the 1760s and 1770s. Building activity had a loosely inverse relationship to martial activity; so when England was fighting she wasn't building houses, as investment was diverted elsewhere. In times of peace and prosperity, construction took off again. The earlier of these two boom periods followed the end of the War of the Spanish Succession (1701–14), then later, the Seven Years War (1756–63).

Supply responded to demand. In London, a second wave of residents moved from the City to the West End, with visitors also expanding the area's population. Lengthier parliamentary sessions brought landed noblemen and gentlemen to Westminster for longer periods than in the previous century. And the 'season' – a series of entertainments, both public and private – ran alongside Parliament in the social calendar for the amusement

not only of MPs but also their wives and families. By the second half of the century, lengthier stays in London meant MPs and their families were increasingly disinclined to make do with temporary lodgings when in the capital, as they had been in the 17th century. They wanted their own houses, whether to rent or to buy.

As in earlier centuries, people also came to London to consult with lawyers, financiers, doctors, architects and other professionals, and to manage their business and property interests. They came to network, with an eye to lucrative government posts, court positions or perhaps military commissions. They came to make money, raise money and, above all, to spend it. The range of goods that people were able to trade in or buy expanded as the century progressed, with exotic imports pouring into the world's greatest seafaring nation from all over the globe. As the century wore on, the streets became better paved and better lit, so that shopping was well accommodated as a leisure pursuit. And as

the 'season' developed, it became sufficient reason in itself to remain in town. Members of the landowning classes might spend as much as seven months of the year in the city – far longer than they ever spent on their country estates. Other London residents lived in town permanently, as they were tied to the metropolis by their business or profession. It became an increasing feature of London life for the country gentleman or nobleman to live side by side in the West End with city-based gentlemen in very similar houses.

With the exception of parliament and the Court, this pattern was followed in many other cities and towns, although on a smaller scale. Many landowners had houses in their county town instead of, or in addition to, a house in the capital. Cities like York also offered other delights to visitors, for example racecourses, while other towns capitalized on natural features, such as spas or the seaside (see pages 80-101). Urban life thrived and architecture responded not only with houses, but with

ABOVE: London life was about more than just parties and other entertainments, but a crush of people at a rout in a town house was all part of urban fun. Here the rout is at the Duchess of Portland's house, as illustrated by Thomas Rowlandson, 1795.

with gusto, catering for all levels of the market. However, the practice was now dominated less by entrepreneurs after a ready fortune and more by aristocratic landowners, who were keen to generate a long-term income from their entailed, town-based estates.

In terms of supply, it was obvious, as demonstrated in the 17th century, that it was simplest and most time- and cost-effective for builders to erect rows of fairly or very similar terraced houses. Nevertheless, building investment needed to respond to a *demand* for houses of this type. This demand was generated not only by the influx of people into towns on a permanent or temporary basis, but also by a further move away from larger houses.

As far as London was concerned, we can make an intelligent guess as to why the large, freestanding town house gave way to the smart terrace, particularly if we look at account books detailing time and money spent in town. It is quite apparent that a town house was very often an unaffordable luxury, which temporarily or permanently rendered even some of the city's loftiest and richest residents paupers. Unlike the country house, or indeed the medieval 'inn', the town house of this era was not self-sufficient, and it was not only costly in itself, but also in the various demands that habitation made on its occupant's purse. There were rooms to be decorated, there was furniture to be bought, a household to be catered for, parties to be thrown and an image to be maintained. The desire to own a house seems to have overridden any concerns about affordability and the concomitant expense to its owner. So while visitors were less prepared to take temporary lodgings, preferring a whole house to themselves, they were also less prepared, or inclined, to spend money on a detached mansion – or even a mansion within a terrace. Contemporary evidence makes clear that larger houses generally did not sell well, and were often subdivided into smaller homes, for which there was a ready market.

ABOVE AND OPPOSITE: *The refurbished front of Fairfax House, York, by John Carr, is a good mid-18th-century example of the type of wider town house owned by prominent men in provincial cities. Inside, the house contains splendid plasterwork and an elegant staircase, here lit by an ample Palladian window.*

a range of new building types for education, health, leisure and entertainment – no self-respecting town was without its assembly hall.

With the exception of Bath (see pages 82-87), urban planning still left a lot to be desired, although some of that desire was gratified as the 18th century progressed, with more architecturally ambitious rows of houses increasingly grouped into squares, crescents and circuses. The speculative building practices that had been established in the 17th century continued

'IN ALL RESPECTS CONVENIENT'

Inside the Town House

The terraced house was admired not just because it was cheaper to build, buy and run, but also because it satisfied the generic needs of town residents. And it seems that its occupants went one step further, liking it for its own peculiar qualities. Thus there was a strong correlation between what was feasible and what was necessary in town.

RIGHT: 23 Bedford Row, London, betrays all the restraint of the early 18th-century house, with plain brickwork and scarcely recessed windows. The façade is saved from dullness by a prominent door hood of the type that was soon to fall victim to fashion and legislation.

As is the case today, 18th-century advertisements for houses reveal the priorities of purchasers and tenants when seeking a property in town. Often, especially in London where space was already at a premium, advertisements for houses in daily and weekly newspapers emphasize the 'convenience' of the residence – especially its 'offices', that is, the kitchens and other practical areas that were essential to the efficient running of the town house. These are mentioned ahead of any reference to more aesthetic features, to which very little attention is paid in these adverts, probably because there was – at least externally – so little distinction between one house and the next. And when new façades are mentioned, it is because they are new and therefore sound, not because they followed a particular design or architectural style.

'Convenience' had two related meanings in this period. In terms of architectural theory, the word was related to a very longstanding principle reiterated by theorists at home and abroad, most notably in France, that every building should be suited to its purpose – meaning both its use and the individuals who were to use it. Analogous terms, more meaningful to modern sensibilities, would be 'fitting' or 'appropriate'. But certainly, in the context

BELOW: Houses in Bedford Square, London, like those at Bedford Row, show how little ornamentation was required to lift a row of houses above the routine. Here, later-18th-century Coade stone ornamentation enlivens the individual façades in a much flatter way, while the central pedimented and stuccoed section allows the group to be read as a unit, too.

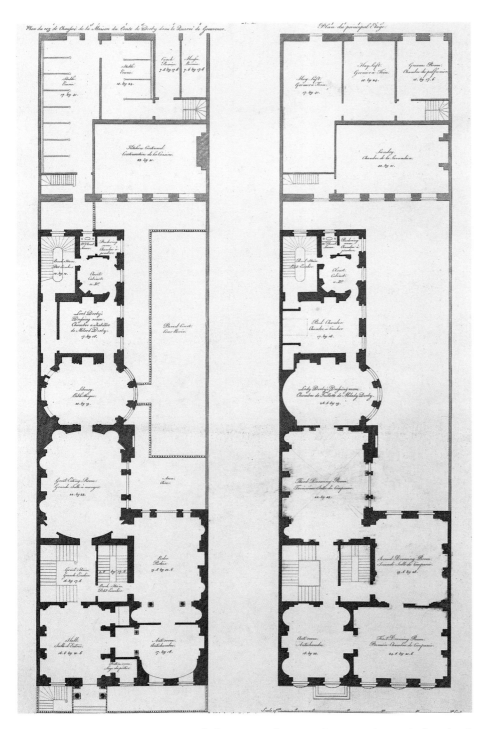

and lived quite happily within them. However, limited space did not preclude lavish entertainments for huge crowds, and the crush of people was sometimes part of the pleasure. The town house could be wholly 'convenient' on its own terms. In fact, in its direct response to its urban conditions, it was the most convenient type of all.

A Typical Terraced House

The 'typical' terraced town house of the late 17th and 18th centuries rose three or four storeys high above a basement storey below ground. The main reception rooms were on the first floor, a level that was often distinguished, in keeping with Palladian precedent, by deeper windows. The dining and family rooms were on the ground floor. The kitchens and other 'offices' were below street level, and were reached by steps at the front of the house. Bedrooms were spread over the second and third floors. Although there was a tendency, as the century progressed, towards an individual or family occupying a whole house rather than simply taking 'rooms', the form of the town house lent itself well to a kind of hierarchical living, whether for single or multiple occupation. The floors of a house could be given over to different tenants, with the 'best' rooms (those on the first floor) rented out at a premium. The cheapest and least desirable rooms were those in the attic or the basement. Services were either provided by a landlady or landlord, or bought in from outside. Unlike the country house, the town house had no need to be self-sufficient: it had all the facilities of the town on its doorstep.

Although the universality of John Summerson's definition of the typical house in the post-fire period has been challenged in recent years, his propositions, as ever, remain broadly true. In its modest manifestation, the house had two rooms, one at the front, the other at the back, and a 'closet' per floor, with a staircase to one side, between or behind the

of the town house, 'convenience' also had its more familiar modern-day meaning, and the terraced house had a duty of convenience both to its builders and its occupants. The formula to which it almost always subscribed was the most 'convenient' answer to the needs of both parties.

The town house had no hope of matching the country house in its size and grandeur, and its owners did not expect it to. Rather, they accepted its limitations

two rooms. The closet was a smaller room projecting to the rear at one side of the house, thereby allowing light to enter the back room as well as the closet wing itself. With plots priced according to street frontage, widths were unlikely to be generous, ranging from about 20 feet (6 metres) to an exceptional 60 feet (18 metres) in the better houses with which we are concerned, so houses extended upwards instead. Extending backwards was a limited option, as the need to admit light to central rooms meant that however much the closet wing was lengthened, it had to remain a wing. The plan could be repeated over two, three, four or even five floors, according to the grandeur of the house. The ubiquity of this plan over the next 200 or more years across the country has made us all familiar with it.

Derby House

Loosely Palladian planning principles of symmetry across one or two axes had little relevance in town. Adverts for houses very often promoted 'two good rooms and a closet per floor', suggesting a fairly standard formula that seems to have satisfied most house buyers and tenants. Larger terraces often exploited their extra capacity with bigger rooms rather than more of them, conforming in essence to the same layout. A comparison of Summerson's plan with the far more ambitious scheme devised by the Adam Brothers, Robert (1728–92) and James (1730–94), for Derby House in Grosvenor Square – refurbished in the mid 1770s at untold but certainly great expense – bears witness to this truth. For what was Derby House but an imaginative and costly variation on the same theme? The long rear wing is just an elaborate, stylish version of the simple closet wing. In fact, in Derby House the Adams remodelled a 50-

year-old house in Grosvenor Square that betrayed nothing of its prestigious location in its original layout. They did not disrupt this layout – after all, the formula was 'convenient' – but elaborated it by manipulating the spaces themselves rather than their relative dispositions. At Derby House, and also at Wynn House, 20 St James's Square, (which was rebuilt by the Adams in the early to mid 1770s), a rare expression of fashion within the terraced-house plan is evident. The neoclassicism of the later 18th century could be expressed in variety in room shapes, reminiscent of real Roman buildings, without disrupting the 'typical' town-house formula. As a result, any one of the plethora of socialite visitors to Derby House experienced twists, turns and changing vistas that were quite contrary to the usual experience of walking *through* a town house, and which were reinforced by a style and exuberance of carefully managed decoration that exceeded anything seen before in town or country.

The other two types of house – the freestanding mansion and the wide-fronted house – were far less restricted by their urban sites, and had little need to respond

OPPOSITE AND ABOVE: *Robert and James Adam's refurbishment of Derby House, Grosvenor Square, London, in the mid 1770s, created sequences of spaces, differently shaped and decorated, to entertain the visitor's eye. The circuit of rooms over two floors was a key part of fashionable entertainment in the later 18th century. Here, the circuit built to a climax in the Third Drawing Room, illustrated in dramatic fashion in the Adams' own Works in Architecture, 1773-74. The degree and type of decorative detail caused Horace Walpole to describe the house as 'filigreed into puerility'.*

to peculiarly urban requirements or constraints in their planning. As such, the plans of new-built houses varied little from those of houses of the equivalent size built in the country, and they were able to reflect the same Palladian planning ideal of symmetry that dictated to their rural counterparts.

A Well-Placed Door

Yet, as we have seen, Palladian principles could scarcely touch the insides of terraced houses. Palladianism could dictate the vertical proportions of their rooms, determined in any case by storey heights that already responded externally to

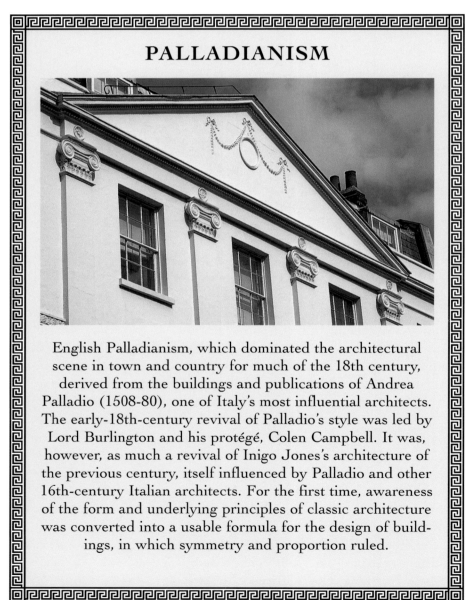

PALLADIANISM

English Palladianism, which dominated the architectural scene in town and country for much of the 18th century, derived from the buildings and publications of Andrea Palladio (1508-80), one of Italy's most influential architects. The early-18th-century revival of Palladio's style was led by Lord Burlington and his protégé, Colen Campbell. It was, however, as much a revival of Inigo Jones's architecture of the previous century, itself influenced by Palladio and other 16th-century Italian architects. For the first time, awareness of the form and underlying principles of classic architecture was converted into a usable formula for the design of buildings, in which symmetry and proportion ruled.

Palladian regimentation. It could govern elements of interior decoration – mini-Palladian elements such as chimneypieces and door cases, niches and screens – but it was pretty much helpless in the face of the planning imperatives of the terraced house. Nevertheless, some designers persisted with Palladian ideals, both in theory and in practice. Notably, the pattern-books that appeared in such large numbers in the 18th century made very few references to terraced houses, and those references that can be found are mostly unflattering. Instead, they persevered with sometimes ludicrously grand designs for town houses that were well beyond the scale of anything that could be accommodated in London and even in most towns beyond. Chief among the more moderate designs is the Palladian-villa type, which is really just the country house brought to town. Such designs make no concessions to the circumstances of urban life, except where they are actually a pretentious mask for two or more terraced houses, which was often the case in practice.

While visually satisfying, in all but the widest house fronts a central entrance was both a planning nonsense and also a challenge to which few designers were prepared to rise, even for the cause of Palladianism. The writer and designer Isaac Ware clung to the ideal of a central doorway in his dismissive writings on the town house, and as a result found himself, theoretically, with a large hall which, as he had argued in the same text, was ridiculous in town. Placing a door in the centre of a façade results in one of two things. The first is a central hallway and rooms disposed either side of a central axis that leads from the house's front to back. This is all very well for Palladian perfection, but thoroughly impractical in a limited urban frontage in that it creates two front rooms of equal but often equally useless proportions. The alternative is to give over the entire house front to a hall, which is just as pointless, as it limits the number of reception rooms by allotting an unnecessarily large amount of space to something (and Ware was correct on this) that scarcely needed to be much of a size at all.

Perhaps where designers thought of the town house as a single unit, as Ware did, rather than a member of a group, they were more likely to opt for a central entrance. The entrance to one side looks especially odd – or incorrect – in an isolated instance. But how often did the tall, thin town house stand alone? There are examples to be seen, but they look as if they are waiting sadly for their neighbours and, as with so much relating to the town house, they often are hostages to economics, rather than aesthetics and design.

ABOVE: John Vardy's pair of houses at Old Palace Yard, Westminster, London, masquerading as a mid-century Palladian country house.

LEFT: This house in Bristol's Great George Street illustrates a theorist's ideal rarely found in the capital's more overcrowded streets: a house wide enough to cope with a central entrance and to present at least an air of detachment.

Ware was not the only designer to cling blindly to the idea of a central entrance; other designers did so, at least on paper, putting the resultant symmetry to good use in pretty, balanced façades – and never mind about the knock-on effect inside. There are two notable built examples, too. William Kent's house for Lady Isabella Finch, at No 44 Berkeley Square (1744–45) relied on a central doorway to achieve a model Palladian appearance, with heavy rustication giving weight and breadth to its narrow façade. Inside, Kent (1684–1748) had no intention of following the 'convenient' town-house plan in any case. Yes, the central entrance creates two half rooms either side at the front, but the house is simply a container for an especially grand staircase and first-floor saloon. Lady Finch required little else in terms of accommodation, and these features are scale models of those found in country houses, rather than direct responses to urban conditions. The central door case is, therefore, beside the point in this instance, in neither dictating nor responding to the house's principal features.

At 1 Bedford Square (c. 1775), Thomas Leverton (not certainly, but most probably) created another exceptional house. It was a commissioned house placed just outside a speculative residential square, and therefore was not obliged to be governed by the architecture within it. It was something like a show house, too, setting up a display unmatched in any other known house of this period in London or beyond, starting with its most unusual façade. Like the earlier house at Berkeley Square, the façade relies on its central entrance for effect, and that entrance has a similar almost military solidity, for all that it is

LEFT: *The unusual doorcase at No 1 Bedford Square, London, reminiscent of a triumphal arch, celebrates the central entrance to an idiosyncratic house.*

OPPOSITE: *Inside No 1 Bedford Square all is sweetness and light, with understated decoration and delightful curves to soften the corners.*

achieved in an entirely different manner appropriate to its period. But internally, the play with room shapes and interior style is both more subtle and more sophisticated than the house at Berkeley Square. It is also very much a town interior, responding to limitations of space and the manner of movement around the house in a way the earlier house did not. The front part of the ground floor, as the central entrance dictates, is given over to hall space, but the architect has contrived to shape three useful spaces out of what is effectively one, with the staircase in the first, on the left; the hall proper in the centre; and an anteroom on the right. Beyond lies the principal ground-floor room, with curving corners and cornices through which the architect seems almost to relish the room's modest proportions. The same subtleties appear at first-floor level, where the central entrance has lost its impact.

Elsewhere in the real world, the doorway to the far left or right bay of a three-bay or even five-bay house prevailed because it simply made more sense. This position allowed for a decent-sized room in the other two bays at the front, and an adequate hall. And as houses were increasingly grouped in uniform rows, sometimes aspiring to the appearance of a 'palace' (see page 60) the placing of the doors in a row's overall design was not an issue anyway, except where they were paired to provide special emphasis, or where the central house of a row was given a wider frontage and a central entrance to provide a focal point and to create some symmetry, not only in the house, but in the terrace as a whole.

But in general, a central entrance was inconvenient, and in its plan the town house rose above the dictates of Palladianism and architectural theories of 'convenience' to settle into a truly convenient formula that endures today.

OPPOSITE: *Limited space carefully manipulated in all dimensions in the entrance hall at No 1 Bedford Square.*

STAIRCASES

The limited space available in the town house made the handling of the staircase of critical importance. While nothing much is made of it in many houses, in others the staircase's inevitable constriction is offset by great attention to decorative detail and the handling of balusters, tread ends and handrails, wherever the staircase can be viewed – whether from above, below or on the stair itself. Stairs were lit by side windows or, increasingly, from a skylight. The attention to detail often petered out at the second-floor landing, beyond which only children, servants and tenants ventured. Skilful architects also manipulated the spaces in which stairs were contained, as can be seen here, at No 1 Bedford Square, and at Home House (see page 70).

SIMILARITY AND DIFFERENCE

The Town House Aesthetic Consolidated

Despite remaining essentially the same as its 17th-century predecessor in arrangement and planning, the 'standard' house began to look a little different on the outside during the second decade of the 18th century. The first building boom coincided handily with the introduction of Palladianism as a kind of default 'style', or, more accurately, design formula. The principles of uniformity and consistency of scale within and between houses had been established and widely displayed during the period of reconstruction after the Great Fire, so that these in themselves were nothing new.

BELOW: Coade stone ornament unites houses at Southernhay West, Exeter, and makes them remarkably similar to earlier houses at Bedford Square, London.

What Palladianism did in this respect was validate and further codify those principles, such that high theory came to govern common practice. Most notably in the case of the town-house façade, Palladianism also shifted the relative proportions of the floors (making the first floor deeper than the ground floor or second floor) and the intervening spaces between the windows and piers. It allowed architects and builders to design to a formula that, while apparently simple, had an intellectual basis for satisfying the eye and mind.

The domestic building booms of the period reinforced the move towards standardization, which we have already seen at work in the later 17th century, not only in building templates but also in ornamental elements. Coade Stone, an artificial stone produced in Lambeth, south London, is the best-known example of the way decorative features were increasingly produced to set designs that were selected from a catalogue. Pattern-books also helped disseminate designs within and between cities and towns, accounting for a great deal of similarity across the country.

Old Burlington Street

During the earlier part of the 18th century the Palladian influence was asserted over new-built houses, particularly in the West End of London. Houses that were built in Old Burlington Street in the 1730s display this formula well, despite the visual impact of later changes to the fronts of many houses. Each of the original façades is fairly plain, with the first floor emphasized not only by deeper windows, but also because it rests on a string course running the width of the house. The visual logic within each individual house derives from the classical column with its pedestal and entablature – the ground floor is the pedestal, the first and second floors form the column and the cornice running below the attic storey is the entablature. That is, the proportions of the individual house façade are governed by orders even though those orders do not make an appearance themselves. Although the windows in the three-bay façades line up under each other in a regular, measured way, there really is no vertical emphasis; instead the string course and cornice provide a horizontal emphasis that is consid-

erably multiplied as they run into and across the neighbouring houses. The whole row would originally have been bound together in this way, not with any pretensions at something grand, but simply to present the row as a unit rather than as several individual houses. This is the early-18th-century Palladian aesthetic at its peak; unsurprisingly, given that the street was laid out in the 1730s by Lord Burlington (1694–1753), champion of Palladianism, and built by his protégés Colen Campbell (1676–1729) and William Kent. The same type of horizontal emphasis can still be seen at nearby Savile Row and numerous other sites within and beyond the capital. These proportions, particularly when repeated over several façades, work against the inherent vertical emphasis of the town house.

The town house, and certainly the classic town house, is almost always a building that is much taller than it is wide. It reaches upwards, piling floor upon floor, and is kept from toppling by its equally lanky neighbours. The Palladian formula, particularly as applied to the whole row and,

ABOVE LEFT AND RIGHT: Horizontality rules the day in Old Burlington Street, London, with emphatic string course and cornice marching across successive façades. The individual houses are marked out only at ground floor level, with appropriately masculine doorcases.

OPPOSITE: An early-18th-century façade betrays nothing of the house beyond, built and altered over several centuries from medieval times onwards. The unusual barley-sugar columns – a Baroque motif rare in England – guard the entrance to Clifton House, Kings Lynn.

BELOW: The Georgian façade comes in all shapes and sizes at King Street, King's Lynn, masking older houses. Such streets are the antithesis of the planned regularity of Old Burlington Street (see previous page).

with the help of emphatic mouldings, worked against the tendency of each individual house to look tall and slim. Instead, each house had to suppress its individual inclinations and join hands with its neighbours to present a united front, based firmly on the ground.

This type of horizontal formula can only really be achieved within an individual, wide building or a row of houses that has been designed as a whole. Its impact rests on mouldings that run relentlessly at the same level across several individual façades, subjugating the individual house to the whole. It creates a kind of uniform, which is most striking *en masse*, in ranks. This style was the single greatest difference between houses of the later 17th and very early 18th century and those of the 1720s to 1750s. The town house of the preceding period, even when in a row, retained something of its lofty nature. It kept ranks with its neighbours, but did not join hands, as its mouldings were less like-

ly to make it do so, at least obtrusively. What is more, window and pier widths were relatively narrow compared with what came later, and pilasters sometimes helped the cause, as did aprons that joined windows vertically so that everything conspired to give an accurate impression of the house's true nature.

The impact of Palladianism, and more loosely classicism, was not limited to new residential developments. Within town centres existing individual houses were either knocked down and rebuilt in the new 'style' or simply given a smart, modern, classical front, bearing little, if any, relation to what it fronted. Many Georgian-looking houses in towns across the country are in fact much earlier in origin, some having gone through a series of additions and re-modellings over a century or more before sticking at an external Georgian elegance. Sometimes the replacement of old-fashioned casement windows with modern sash windows was

enough to elevate older housing to an acceptable modern level; advertisements for houses in late 18th-century York certainly emphasize sash windows as a desirable feature, perhaps to distinguish the modern or modernized house from the bulk of older, old-fashioned housing.

The English Urban Renaissance

In that context, it certainly seems that provincial town-house owners viewed a Palladian façade as a sign of good taste and status. The historian Peter Borsay links the rise of urban domestic Palladianism with middle-class ambition within what he terms the 'English urban renaissance'. While classicizing façades of new terraces in cities and towns resulted in very few distinctions between houses, the individual classical façade applied to one unit in a row of older buildings set a house and its occupant apart from the lower classes living in vernacular buildings. The classicism of the 17th century

SASH WINDOWS

The sash window, formed of sliding frames running in vertical grooves, appeared in England in the late 17th century, and soon replaced hinged casement windows in all but the humblest building stock. In earlier sash windows, only one frame moved; in later ones, both moved. As the 18th century progressed, the glazing bars became more slender and the panes of glass grew larger. The availability of sheet glass in the 19th century reduced the window to two large panes, greatly affecting the relationship between window divisions and the divisions of the building front as a whole, and certainly working to the detriment of the classic town house's appearance.

THE PALACE FRONT

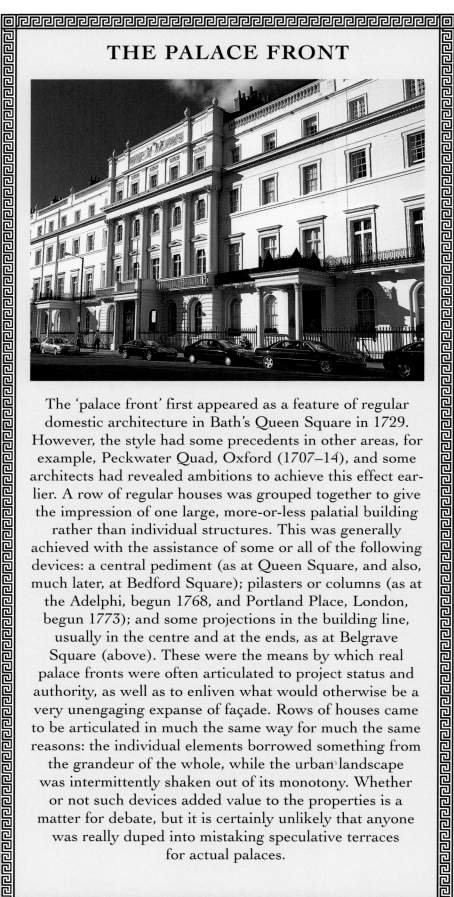

The 'palace front' first appeared as a feature of regular domestic architecture in Bath's Queen Square in 1729. However, the style had some precedents in other areas, for example, Peckwater Quad, Oxford (1707–14), and some architects had revealed ambitions to achieve this effect earlier. A row of regular houses was grouped together to give the impression of one large, more-or-less palatial building rather than individual structures. This was generally achieved with the assistance of some or all of the following devices: a central pediment (as at Queen Square, and also, much later, at Bedford Square); pilasters or columns (as at the Adelphi, begun 1768, and Portland Place, London, begun 1773); and some projections in the building line, usually in the centre and at the ends, as at Belgrave Square (above). These were the means by which real palace fronts were often articulated to project status and authority, as well as to enliven what would otherwise be a very unengaging expanse of façade. Rows of houses came to be articulated in much the same way for much the same reasons: the individual elements borrowed something from the grandeur of the whole, while the urban landscape was intermittently shaken out of its monotony. Whether or not such devices added value to the properties is a matter for debate, but it is certainly unlikely that anyone was really duped into mistaking speculative terraces for actual palaces.

was a start, but Palladianism brought with it a set of rules that ensured a distinction between those who knew how house design should be done, and those who did not. Classical urban architecture, both civic and domestic, was certainly an expression of success, even if it was achieved in some less-than-admirable fields. For example, Bristol's classic town houses, terraces and squares reflected the city's mercantile success, most particularly as a result of the slave trade.

In towns where there was no space, demand or finance for building a unified row, the palace front (see box) was the most usual manifestation of 'classical' style rather than classic town house. Such houses were also individual commissions, whereas much of the classicizing architecture in towns, as we have seen, was the product of speculative development. Although most speculative houses subscribed to the lowest common denominator of Palladian town-house design, a ground landlord or other speculator might aim a little higher with ambitions to aggrandize a new development. The blessing of such schemes was that they did not need to disturb the nature of the individual houses that fell within the project, while between them they could aspire to some overarching Palladian correctness in a joint façade. Externally, the individual houses at Bedford Square, London, followed the basic Anglo-Palladian town-house format; the essentially plain, brick façades with uniform proportions were enlivened and somewhat distinguished by different degrees of ornamentation in Coade Stone and, in some cases, stucco. These units were then grouped together, with central pediments on each side, in a loose imitation of a long palace façade. In both respects, it was a simple idea that was used to good effect, despite the architectural solecism of an odd number of pilasters 'supporting' the pediment on the north and south sides. However, the function of the 'palace front' was not to dupe observers or purchasers into believing this

was a square of only four extensive mansions rather than over 50 three-bay houses. The applications of Coade Stone and stucco distinguish the individual houses and articulate each row, countering the potential monotony of a terrace of identical houses, while adding – through a pervading neatness as much as anything – a certain cachet to the whole development.

Rediscovering the Vertical

Outside of Bath, which took the lead in this matter, it took some time for 'palace fronts' to get off the page and into the town, and by the time this came about, a new and absolutely antithetical movement was afoot, particularly in London. The vertical emphasis embraced by designers in the post-fire period, and subsequently suppressed in the Palladian era, was rediscovered and celebrated by some of the leading architects of the second half of the 18th century, a time when the architecture of the town house really came into its own. This rediscovery coincided with the 'neoclassical' age, and particularly the age of

the 'Adam style'. Following the mid-century excavations at Herculaneum and Pompeii, architects and other designers had an astonishing array of 'authentic' decorative devices at their disposal, which derived from discoveries made among the ruins of the classical buildings at those sites and elsewhere. When translated into English, these classical features were often expressed through two-dimensional and flat decoration, rather than applied in a three-dimensional, architectonic manner. These influences were rendered in paint, plaster or stucco that was simply applied to an interior or exterior surface and had little impact on the form or nature of the surface itself. Such flatness suited the town house: fire-wary building regulations ensured that new-built houses were rid of the ornamental projections, such as carved door hoods, which had enlivened individual house façades and distinguished them from others in previous eras. More regulation at this point – in the form of the 1774 Building Act – took previous legislation further, encouraging even flatter façades

ABOVE: The ashlar-faced houses at 47-51 Friar Gate, Derby, join forces and pretend to be one large house – an old trick by this time. The neat double porches and ground floor windows with extra side panels are the only clue to a late-Georgian date.

BELOW: Robert Adam's 1772 design for Wynn House, 20 St James's Square, London, is an abstraction of the temple front made to suit the individual town-house façade. The elements are shallow in profile, celebrating the house's inherent linearity.

with scarcely any scope for all but the very flattest, most physically reticent decoration, at least when fashioned from flammable materials. But things were moving that way anyway. As before, the legislation codified things that were already happening. Robert Adam's design for the elevation to 20 St James's Square (1771–74) is a fine example of neoclassical ornament used to enliven a façade – Palladian proportion here gave way to the need to stretch the first floor to accommodate an

elaborate barrel-vaulted ceiling in the front room, a more unusual example of neoclassicism taking a three-dimensional form in the town house. Adam's work here is a free interpretation of the classy stone temple front that James Stuart (1712–88) had earlier added to No 15 in the same square (1764–6), but it is still more suited both to the tall, narrow town house and to the fashion for flat finery on house façades.

Architects like Robert Adam and James Paine (1745–1829) set individual town-house fronts free again. Although not everybody wished to spend money on a differentiated front, there are many surviving designs from this period – some realized and others not – that reveal a new aesthetic at work. Robert Adam's designs for 11 St James's Square and George Dance's unexecuted design for 6 St James's Square are excellent examples. Each celebrates the verticality and discreteness of the individual building. Dance (1741–1825) achieved this by lining up windows in two strips flanked by pilasters, the outer of which joins with a second pilaster at each level to clearly mark the limits of the house. Adam countered the horizontality of a five-bay house by emphasizing its three middle bays, with an elegant, lofty configuration of pilasters that drew attention away from the boundaries of the house and into its centre. It is significant, of course, that all these houses were refurbishments of older buildings, in that they did not need to conform to the governing aesthetic of a new row or square. By comparison, St James's Square shows evidence of earlier, less successful designs, notably Edward Shepherd's work at No 4 (1726–28), where the heavy mouldings and expanse of brickwork above the first-floor windows make the front look squat or rather unhappily slumped.

A Lack of Distinction

Despite being refined into its classic form in this century, the town house was the

subject of much casual and formal criticism. At the root of this criticism lay four things: a real and understandable concern with the speed and scale of development; concerns about construction standards; a rather unrealistic ambition to see the town house as the ornament and pride of the city and country; and what now seems a rather snobbish and illogical obsession with appropriateness and legibility.

Both the 'rage of building' and how it was manifested prompted such writers as John Gwynn and John Stewart to write essays on London's architectural planning (or lack of it) and development, in which they criticized the form that London's houses were taking by default. They saw an opportunity going to waste and felt qualified to offer their own suggestions and solutions.

John Stewart found it hard to credit that noblemen would be happy living in a terraced house; and as more members of the lesser gentry and the middling classes were set on occupying if not owning a house in town, there was a good chance that those noblemen and women would also be living next door to people much less noble than themselves. Stewart's observation was tinged with disappointment that this should be the case; he would have much preferred that noblemen built splendid freestanding mansions that would ornament the city. But not only did mansions cost even more money, adequate plots in town and city centres were often scarce and, it seems, such mansions were simply not fashionable. As we have seen, very few large detached houses were built in London in the 18th century, and, certainly, by the second half of the century, even the wealthiest purchasers were showing a positive preference for a grand or even modest terraced house.

At the root of Stewart's complaints was the concern that pervaded later 18th-century society: if everyone dressed the same and their houses looked the same (at least from outside) how could one tell who was who, or more particularly, who was what?

Given that there were essentially few, if any, distinctions between the houses of the nobleman and the professional, for example, the town house was an ostensibly classless product in an age obsessed with class, rank and distinction. While we might perceive this as a virtue in the 21st century, many 18th-century men and women would not have agreed. We should not take the strongly voiced objections to be too representative, however. Even the critics must have lived in these houses and

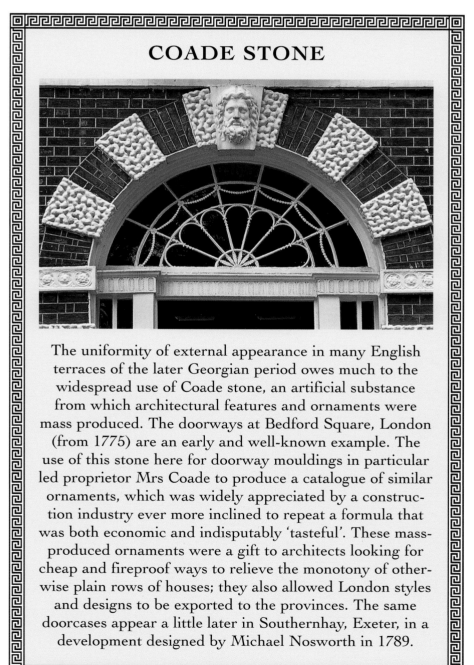

COADE STONE

The uniformity of external appearance in many English terraces of the later Georgian period owes much to the widespread use of Coade stone, an artificial substance from which architectural features and ornaments were mass produced. The doorways at Bedford Square, London (from 1775) are an early and well-known example. The use of this stone here for doorway mouldings in particular led proprietor Mrs Coade to produce a catalogue of similar ornaments, which was widely appreciated by a construction industry ever more inclined to repeat a formula that was both economic and indisputably 'tasteful'. These mass-produced ornaments were a gift to architects looking for cheap and fireproof ways to relieve the monotony of otherwise plain rows of houses; they also allowed London styles and designs to be exported to the provinces. The same doorcases appear a little later in Southernhay, Exeter, in a development designed by Michael Nosworth in 1789.

ADAM STYLE

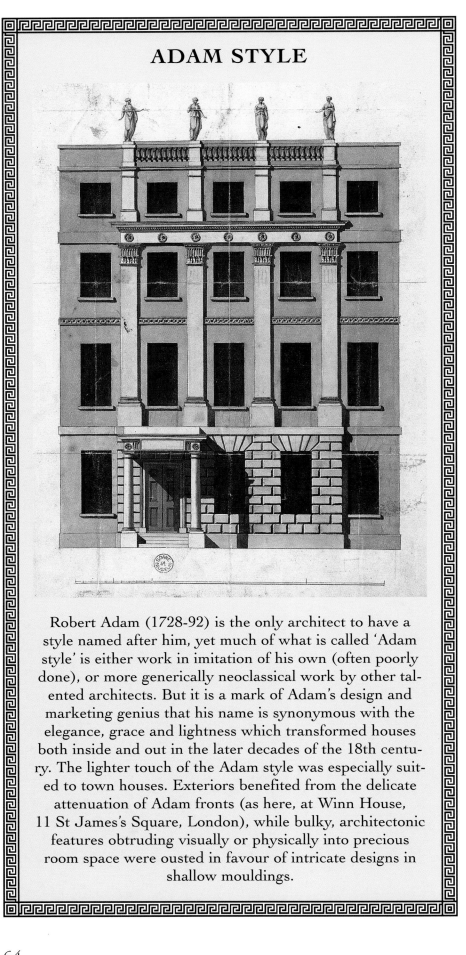

Robert Adam (1728-92) is the only architect to have a style named after him, yet much of what is called 'Adam style' is either work in imitation of his own (often poorly done), or more generically neoclassical work by other talented architects. But it is a mark of Adam's design and marketing genius that his name is synonymous with the elegance, grace and lightness which transformed houses both inside and out in the later decades of the 18th century. The lighter touch of the Adam style was especially suited to town houses. Exteriors benefited from the delicate attenuation of Adam fronts (as here, at Winn House, 11 St James's Square, London), while bulky, architectonic features obtruding visually or physically into precious room space were ousted in favour of intricate designs in shallow mouldings.

though they may have considered them a necessary evil, there were many more who thought of them more positively.

Gwynn shared Stewart's concerns about a lack of legibility in housing stock. He envisioned the classes as integrated yet distinguished, with the more distinctive houses of the nobility operating as high points or landmarks among the undifferentiated, tastefully uniform houses of the gentry and middling classes. Bedford Square came too late for his assessment, but he might have approved: there was some correlation between house and status among the first occupants, with the two titled residents in the larger, central houses on the east and west sides. But it was essentially a middle-class square, and the other two pediments bridged two regular houses first occupied by a reverend, a director of the South Sea Company and two other non-titled gentlemen.

Distinction between houses generally occurred on the inside, with greater or lesser expressions of fashion. To us, the contrast between the very plain façade of Derby House and its elaborate interior is harder to reconcile than the lack of external contrast between one house and another. But it was an extreme example of the 18th-century tendency to save the best for the interior, for private view, even if the outsider in the street could glimpse some grandeur through the elongated first-floor windows.

Complaints from the likes of Stewart and Gwynn were aimed very much at our 'classic' English town house. Wider, provincial houses reflected their occupant's prestige with their size and appearance. At the same time they could be symmetrical in façade and plan – more properly 'classical' – and they could ornament a town. Nevertheless, the provinces were often behind the times, as it took a while for fashions to permeate from London to other towns and cities. So while we see splendid examples of the wide-fronted town house, with a central door and more scope for architectural play, in style these

houses are often rather retrograde. This is often true of provincial terraces, too: when Blandford was rebuilt after a serious fire in 1731, it adopted the style of the later 17th century rather than the Palladianism that was well and truly established in London and Bath by that time.

I would argue, in any case, that these broader houses sit somewhat outside our definition of the 'classic'. Wider houses are 'classic' only in the sense of being, at times, classical. They lack the vertical emphasis that I uphold to be the essence of the classic English town house's aesthetic appeal. And that aesthetic appeal seems to excuse, or even cause us to relish, the peculiar disposition of rooms over several storeys inside. The link between contingency and response seems to dictate the aesthetic. It is almost as if the classic English town house is defined by its response to contingencies, and we delight in those contingencies and responses for their own sake. The town house may fail by universal standards, but when done well it excels by its own.

If noblemen did not intend to provide great architecture in town in the form of freestanding mansions, then the next best thing, the critics stated, was neatness. Writers commentating on what London's architecture could or should be often express a general desire for uniformity, which they equate with beauty. Gwynn envisioned 'London and Westminster improved' through greater attention to planning, uniformity and elegance. Bath was by no means perfect, especially in Gwynn's eyes (see page 69), but at least the dominance of the two John Woods, father and son, led to a tighter rein and

ABOVE: More provincial glory at Peckover House, Wisbech, built shortly before 1727. In style it is slightly behind its times, with brick dressings, a large segmental pediment over its Tuscan doorcase and segment-headed windows, which are the same depth on the first and second floors and unevenly, if symmetrically, disposed.

65

ABOVE: *A window in Bath puts local stone to good use in this elegant composition.*

bolder statements there than were generally apparent in London. Development in the metropolis was more piecemeal and less subject to the overall vision and control of a particular architect, builder or developer. The Bedford Estate worked hard to maintain both standards and uniformity, with a good deal of success. Bedford Square was praised by another writer in 1783 as 'a proof of the improvement of our taste' with 'the regularity and symmetry of the sides … the great breadth of the pavements and the neatness of the iron rails'. Not much to ask for, it seems, but often hard to achieve, especially where different builders developed plots in groups of two or three.

Sometimes non-aesthetic interests lay behind the call for tidiness in urban domestic architecture. Real and perceived links between the untidy and the threateningly dirty certainly contributed to the implementation of urban planning in the 18th century and beyond. Neat houses set out in neat rows in neat streets and squares would be not only inoffensive, but also hygienic.

Putting on a Front

The 'rage of building' threatened to sweep every green field out of its way as the City of London and Westminster burst their bounds. As with any situation that is both unprecedented in scale and seemingly out of control, this 'rage' caused great anxiety in itself. The speed with which buildings were erected with the aim of making money rather than providing effective

LEFT: *A quadrant of houses at the Circus, in Bath, sweeps round to greet the next, in one of the most successful attempts at turning speculative housing into a work of art.*

architecture also led to justified anxiety about the quality of construction. Construction practices were at their shoddiest within the speculative business in which the vast majority of town houses were built. Stories abound of houses tumbling into streets before they were even finished. No doubt some of these tales are apocryphal, but there must have been more than a grain of truth in them. Existing evidence certainly makes it clear that construction methods, even in some of the better areas, left much to be desired. Architectural theorist and architect Isaac Ware dubbed this slack practice with a view to a quick and substantial profit the 'art of slight building', and the architect James Peacock considered the master of the 'art' to be the builder who could erect

a house with just enough strength for it to remain standing until sold. Surveys of some 18th-century terraced houses do reveal a disconcerting lack of either the ability or the willingness to build soundly, with the outer walls of houses barely connected to the inner shell and the weaker bricks carrying the bulk of the load.

London attracted most of the criticism, but Bath – another city changed beyond recognition by intense and prolonged building activity during the 18th century – received its fair share of complaints. Like London, Bath was visited by people of all classes from many parts of the country, and as such was very much in the public eye, as we see in the next chapter (see pages 82-87). In the novel *Humphry Clinker* (1771), Tobias Smollett's Squire Bramble

ABOVE: *The Adam brothers' Royal Terrace at the Adelphi, London, long since dispatched, used little more than decorative pilasters to turn a plain rank of terraced houses into a 'palace'. Engraving published in* The Works in Architecture of Robert and James Adam, vol. III, *1822.*

finds 'nothing but disappointment at Bath', where 'the rage of building has laid hold on such a number of adventurers, that one sees new houses starting up in every outlet and every corner of Bath; contrived without judgment, executed without solidity'. Such shoddy construction practice is, of course, not peculiar to the Georgian age, but its manifestation in unsound town houses gave the latter a bad name in their own time. It is particularly ironic that the iconic city of Bath, seat of Georgian domestic architectural perfection in our eyes, should have been the target of such abuse.

In real life, Elizabeth Montagu remarked of Bath houses that she would 'be stifled if the Masonry was not so bad as to admit winds at many places', and also regretted that what on the outside seemed a 'good stone Edifice' was inside nothing more than 'a nest of boxes'. That the terrace's external appearance was at odds

with its internal disposition gave full expression to the term 'putting on a front'. The classic English town house generally presents its smartest face to the street, no matter what expression that face might pull. Although some houses had more elaborate and inventive rear façades, these were generally reserved for plots wide enough to warrant such inventiveness and large enough to accommodate a decent-sized garden from which to appreciate it. Otherwise, the front was usually more elaborate than the rear, even if only marginally – an additional string course might be the only distinction between them. As hundreds of rows of later 18th- and 19th-century houses attest, house fronts were often enlivened or 'made up' as contemporary, and later critics would insinuate, with bright white stucco. A parapet above the cornice, masking the un-classical pitched but very English roof behind, added to the appearance of a smart or smartish front, with imitation or occasionally real stone simply stuck on an otherwise nondescript brick terrace. This matters little, aesthetically, except at the terrace ends, where stucco with mouldings meets brick without, and disrupts the illusion of a neat 'stone' whole.

What is more, while house fronts obeyed the Palladian rules with a balanced disposition of openings, the rear ends of houses did nothing of the sort: windows were sized and placed as required and not to satisfy aesthetic ambitions. A closet wing ruined all hopes of balance in any case. Now this lack of continuity between front and back might seem logical to us, from an economic point of view if not an aesthetic one. It may even add something to the charm of the 18th-century town house. But it incensed some critics who rather naïvely wanted more from the town house than it was ever going to give. Most notably, John Gwynn was saddened and angered by the higgledy-piggledyness of terrace backs letting the side down in his battle for more respectably monumental town architecture. Terraces were not always viewed from the front, he pointed out, and therefore their sides and backs needed the same kind of attention as their street façades. But this was never going to happen. Gwynn's complaints that the splendid houses in the Circus at Bath 'offended' the spectator when he found them to be 'only a heap of confused irregular buildings' at the back was beside the point – people came to Bath for the waters and the society. The general stage set created by the fronts of the various terraces was sufficient backdrop against which to pursue those interests, and assured visitors of all classes that they were participating in something genteel.

The Anti-Adam Brigade

Given the calls for some distinctive grandeur in domestic architecture, it may seem paradoxical that the town house was subject to criticism not only when it appeared in bland, uniform rows, but also

when special efforts had been made to its external decoration. Surely that was what its critics wanted? Apparently not. The type of decoration applied to the fashionable town house in the later 18th century was considered by some to be both tacky in its substance, in that it was only stuck on, and in its appearance. Again, London architects and houses attracted the bulk of the criticism. Work by the Adam brothers or in their style was particularly singled out for criticism. In the early 19th century, Robert Smirke and William Porden talked disparagingly of the way that Robert Adam had 'speckled' London with 'white

ABOVE: A reminder of the Adelphi's glory, in Adam Street, London, shows the kind of 'feminine' applied decoration which some critics thought unseemly on a house front.

ABOVE: *A display plate of the staircase at Home House, London, presents Robert Adam's urban elegance and inventiveness at its peak.*

ABOVE RIGHT: *The shallow profile of delicate plasterwork at No 1 Bedford Square, London, illustrates the light touch of the neo-classical interior in town.*

walls' that were 'no better than Models for the Twelfth-Night-Decoration of a Pastry Cook'. No doubt the Adams shouldered the burden of criticism arising from poor imitations of their style as much, if not more so, than from their own work. Nevertheless, the 'façadism' of which the Adam or Adam-style finish was an example *was* insubstantial, and even the Adams' patented Liardet cement stucco was known to fall off. The widow of the famous actor David Garrick despaired because his will obliged her to keep the house built for him by the Adams in good repair, and a good portion of her widow's allowance was used up doing just this, as the stucco kept coming off. The town house was guilty of a very surface approach to classicism – and this is true, too, of classically re-fronted houses in

provincial towns with medieval remains lurking behind.

The association of external display with commercial interests was apparent in the pre-fire period, notably at Sparrowe's House in Ipswich (see pages 30-31), Sir Paul Pindar's house in Holborn (see pages 23-24), and still earlier at the Jew's House, Lincoln (see page 18). Promotion of one-self, one's property and one's business or trade were closely interlinked, and the elaborate house front could draw attention to all three. The meaner approaches to house façades that were dictated by the need to build quickly in the period following the Great Fire and by the economic interests of such speculative builders as Nicholas Barbon (1640–98) were also perhaps a reflection of the gathering trend that separated residential premises from

business. A merchant trading in the City was increasingly likely to reside in or near the West End, with a house and habits at least externally indistinguishable from that of the nobleperson living next door to him. Is this longstanding connection between external display and commerce (and therefore the middling classes) one reason why fronts such as those the Adams gave to the Royal Terrace, Adelphi and Fitzroy Square were so heavily criticized and in such scathing terms? Horace Walpole described the former as being nothing more than 'warehouses, laced down the seam, like a soldier's trull in a regimental old coat'. As well as making an obvious link with the trappings of trade, Walpole was also attacking the building for what he considered its inappropriately fine, 'feminine' and flimsy ornamentation, and

its inherent deceit in using that finery to disguise its true, utilitarian nature.

The type of decoration that the Adams and others applied to individual houses and particularly to rows was not dissimilar to that used by designers of shop fronts at that time, reinforcing the connections between 'feminine' decoration and commercial interests. But this was not the only reason why such fronts were criticized. Although Walpole's remarks were couched in very personal and telling language, they are very close to that long-held architectural theory that the ornamentation of a building should be appropriate to its use and inhabitant. This advice was usually expressed in the rather clumsy and unhelpful linking of architectural order, that is Ionic or Corinthian, with the status of the person for whom a

ABOVE: *The panelled walls of the bedroom at the early-18th-century Handel House, Brook Street, London.*

71

ABOVE: *The Drawing Room at Pickford's House, Derby, built by Joseph Pickford for himself in the late 1760s, reminds us that 'Adamized' interiors were not as pervasive as their critics suggested.*

residence was being built, presupposing a grand type of residence in the first place. Understandably, it was the general principle rather than its specific application that was most usually heeded. Basically, houses and people should not pretend to be what they were not. Or, to put it another way, a person looking at a house should be able to make an accurate judgement of its occupant's status by that house's exterior. Of course, as we have seen, such theory flew out of the window in the face of the terrace of houses occupied by people of a variety of backgrounds and classes. What would be an appropriate form of decora-

tion? If one was to apply an order to the building, what should it be? Surely no town-house architect, let alone a jobbing speculative developer, would have cared a hoot for such niceties. But there is always some non-practitioner to criticize practice.

Perhaps the Adams' fancy pilasters at the Adelphi, which so irked Walpole, were a new answer to a new problem, inventive genius born of the licence of a new decorative free-for-all in the face of a lack of precedent? Or perhaps they were simply a relatively cheap and easy means of articulating what Walpole rightly identified as a long, warehouse-like façade? Whatever the case, this type of decoration offended on another front: it was considered inappropriate to the exterior of a building. Another long-standing precept was that a building's exterior should have an appropriately 'masculine' demeanour – for which read balanced, solid, sober, controlled, reasonable and rational. 'Feminine' decoration – for which read irrational, giddy, insubstantial and superficial – should be reserved for the interior, where even a man could let himself go, architecturally. The Adelphi pilasters, to borrow Walpole's analogy, were like strips of lace, stuck on to prettify the building and by no means essential to or even suggestive of its substantiality. Instead, they undermined any pretensions to decent, workaday honesty that the building might otherwise have had.

To us, such criticism seems nitpicking and almost ludicrous. Speculative building is commerce. The Adelphi stood out in a competitive market, viewed not only from across the Thames but also from the heavy commercial traffic on the river itself. If its architects saw similarities between their building and the seaside Palace of the Roman Emperor Diocletian, which Robert had earlier 'excavated' in Split, Dalmatia, they were surely sufficiently realist to recognize that this was not how the buying public would perceive it and that the similarities were, in any case, rather loose. The fancy finish simply drew attention to their project and distinguished it from the crowd. Ironically, this distinction was not enough for the houses to sell well, and the Adams made a substantial loss on them, partly recouped through a lottery, in true 18th-century fashion.

As I have said, the Adams were particularly susceptible to criticism, not simply because of their 'offences' against architectural propriety, but also because they were widely and often poorly imitated. As a result, they carried the burden of their imitators' sins as well as their own. What's more, these imitations, being on townhouse exteriors, were as publicly evident as

the originals. However, while there is no evidence that a fancy finish, or, indeed, a palace front, increased the marketability or value of a row of houses, there is also no reason to believe that house buyers stood by some puritan principles of reticence and honesty in all things external and shunned any house dressed in the 'Adam style'.

To the critics, however, the 'faults' of the town house were evidence of an attention to appearance above substance, and while this may have been a pervasive attitude in the 18th century, it was nevertheless (or consequently) one that caused concern. But whether such criticism is

ABOVE: The Dining Room at Pickford's House shows an elegant but unfussy interior that is typical of its time.

ABOVE: *Beyond the capital there was more scope for the bow window, as seen here on a late-18th-century front in Stamford.*

OPPOSITE: *The Music Room at Handel House, in London, with panelling painted in understated but authentic colours.*

What other town-house traits fell foul of the architectural critics and theorists in this period? Like light-hearted exterior decoration, the bow window had overtones of commerce, and what is more, it was ubiquitous and almost always misplaced if the critics are to be believed: although its chief role was to capitalize on a view, it was more likely to be placed, the critics determined, where there was no prospect to be had. However, many leasehold contracts forbade the inclusion of bow windows on a street front, for reasons that are not clear, thereby reinforcing the flatness that is a chief characteristic of our classic town-house façade. Bows to the rear of the building, reflecting and accommodating a trend from the 1760s for shaped rooms, sit more easily with our defined classic town-house aesthetic, where the building's chief delights are hidden from public view.

Internally, the town-house aesthetic also reached its peak in this period. I have already mentioned the elaborate work of the Adam brothers, but the planning of the Derby and Wynn houses was exceptional, displaying a fashion that very few could afford, or would, perhaps, feel inclined to follow. Nevertheless, the internal finishes that the Adam brothers applied to some of their major town houses demonstrate a general tendency towards flat, non-architectonic décor found in town houses of the second half of the 18th century. Their interiors were exceptional in cost, too, but it was nevertheless easy to express modishness in interior decoration and furnishings, which could easily be replaced by a subsequent owner wanting to make his or her mark on what was likely otherwise to be an undistinguished house. Fashionable decoration could be limited to ceilings and fireplaces in the best rooms, and also to mirrors and select pieces of furniture. Not all houses reflected wealth or fashions, and many retained the understated decoration of earlier houses, or were newly decorated in a classy, less fussy style.

justified or not, this 'façadism' is also very much part of the town-house aesthetic. To us, of course, the town house façade is an indicator of what is behind, not because of any physical relation between façade and plan (other than a door to one side), but because we can conceive what lies behind, we know we like it and we hope we're going to find it. In this respect, the 'Georgianized' provincial medieval or Tudor town house is the most deceptive and potentially disappointing of all.

'DESIRABLY SITUATE'

The Town-House Environment

As today, the keywords when looking for a house in any town during the Georgian period were 'location, location, location'. Given that the better building stock was broadly the same, *where* a house was mattered as much as *what* it was. Easy access to sites of business and pleasure was important, given that those were so often the reason for being in town in the first place. Within locations, purchasers might nitpick about the pros and cons of different houses, but the environment in which the town house was situated was often the key to general satisfaction.

BELOW: 'Mrs Congreve with her children', by Philip Reinagle, 1782, shows an interior that is reliant upon a lush carpet and paintings for its colour. The olive walls are a fitting and not uncommon backdrop.

Much of the neat grandeur of the classic English town house depended on behind-the-scenes activity, which was often far less salubrious. The owners of the horses and carriages that transported the wealthier inhabitants of urban areas needed suitable accommodation close to the town house itself, preferably within the confines of its site. Ideally, stabling was at the far end of a residence, with private access from both the house and a mews road behind. The next best option was to hire stabling in a

block as near to home as possible.

Likewise, owners could only get away with a house of limited size because of a hinterland of lesser houses and shops providing servants and services. So, while the better streets and squares politely presented their well-mannered and well-dressed faces to each other, they turned their rough-and-ready backs on ruder buildings and people huddled round every corner. By the end of the 18th century, earlier dreams of squares, neat or grand, adorning our cities were beginning to become reality, at least in London and, as we'll see, spa and seaside towns (see pages 80-101). The town house grouped with its friends in a square created its own environment, forming a community looking in on itself much as the earlier medieval inns had done.

Fashions in the landscaping of squares changed through the century and beyond, but the general purpose was to provide a semi-private space where members of the exclusive community could enjoy the outdoors without much fear of disturbance by non-members. Some, such as Bedford Square, were privately policed at their entrances to vet those wishing to gain access. Others guarded central gardens with railings and locked gates. Nevertheless, city squares were not always as urbane as we might imagine. Certainly earlier in the century, as views of the Royal Crescent at Bath and Berkeley Square in London attest, the areas in front of smart urban developments were often populated by sheep and other livestock, as well as gentlemen and ladies. Although scarcely mentioned in advertisements for houses, views onto well-kept squares must have counted for something in the town-house market. Private gardens are rarely mentioned, too, but while a pretty square offered some compensation for a typically small garden, the 18th and early 19th centuries did produce a range of publications

BELOW: *George Scharf's mid-19th century sketch of the mews behind Torrington Square shows the bustle behind the scenes in the London square, where less salubrious activities supported the sophisticated lives within the houses themselves.*

RIGHT: *An early-18th-century image of Golden Square, London, from a series by Sutton Nicholls. The layout of the central area is unimaginative, but not untypical. Greenery became more important as the century wore on. A closer look at the individual houses belies the initial appearance of uniformity.*

on garden design, planting and maintenance, notably in J C Loudon's *Hints on the Formation of Gardens and Pleasure Grounds* (1812). As previously mentioned, where the size of a garden warranted it, and budget permitted, the rear façade of a town house was sometimes given some architectural attention, so that both garden and the aspect fronting it were worth looking at.

A Pleasing Prospect

What comprised a 'pleasing prospect' was open to debate, but it could include a 'natural' rural view or a manmade urban one. Although a rural 'prospect' was hardly what one came to town for, house adverts in London do mention views out to open countryside and distant hills in what are now the suburbs, where those were to be had. It is hard to imagine now, even outside London, how urban streets and squares built on what we would now call greenfield sites looked out to hills and ended abruptly in fields. Images of this odd juxtaposition of the decidedly urban

and the emphatically rural show not only livestock grazing, but also haymaking and other rural activities. Of course, the town and its inhabitants depended heavily on this activity and its produce. Nevertheless, the culture clash seems particularly severe to a modern-day viewer used to seeing towns tail off into suburban architecture before breaking out into the countryside.

This juxtaposition was not necessarily demanded, either, as it might well mean that one's immediate town-house surroundings were little more than a building site and some rough, muddy roads. It was considered far better to be part of a nicely finished and wholly urban development that was untroubled by the rude environment from which it was fashioned. A pleasing prospect often comprised a view onto other houses that were externally finished in a similar fashion to one's own. If the appearance of these neighbouring houses was attractive and fashionable – or at least neat – so much the better. In fact, the classic town house was itself the greatest contributor to the urban prospect that its neighbours valued.

CONCLUSION
The Town House Excels

The classic English town house, built in its thousands in the Georgian period, is a sign of its times. Everything about it speaks of the speed and economics of urban development and of new approaches to construction and production, which jointly caused so many houses and rows to look the same. The town house of this period displays the overwhelming taste for classicism, even in its most stripped-down mode, the passion for urban life, and the popularity of the town house itself, in its new 'classic' form.

BELOW: Ionic columns are set into the façade at London's Mecklenburgh Square to preserve the 'flat' aesthetic, which was at its peak in the late 18th and early 19th centuries.

Restrictions governing its design were seen by some theorists and designers as preventing the town house from taking any ideal form, as the less-restricted country house could. But there was no denying that it excelled on its own terms; its shape was 'ideal' for the urban circumstances in which it had developed, and in which it now reached its peak. Our classic belongs firmly to the 18th century, owing something to both the earlier and the later parts of the century. The first gave it satisfying proportions and ubiquity, the one reinforcing the effect of the other. The second gave it its own identity and style. Externally it need no longer be understated, even if it often was. The Adam brothers and others had carved out an idiosyncratic style for the town house in which it could dress up at will, while still benefiting from the aesthetic 'rightness' of its Palladian foundation garments. The more adventurous later 18th-century designers did not disrupt the town-house aesthetic in terms of either façades or planning; they maximized it and freed it from the constraints of conformity to an ideal established in another realm altogether, the country house. The next century would further embrace the true nature of the town house, although the style in which it sometimes did so was far removed from the 'classic'.

CHAPTER THREE

A CHANGE OF SCENE

Health, Leisure and the Georgian Town House

The spa and seaside towns of the 18th and early 19th centuries have a special place in the story of the English town house. On the one hand, the particular physical, economic and social circumstances of their architectural creation meant that they often manifested what could only be fantasized about elsewhere – even in London. On the other hand, by reaching out for light and air with bay and bow windows, balconies and verandahs, these structures disrupted the classic town-house aesthetic in a variety of ways, some more successful than others. As we have already seen, the classic English town house is very much the result of the constraints of its evolution; in that respect, the licence offered by virgin sites – particularly at the seaside – did not always work in its favour. Nonetheless, some of the most imaginative, idiosyncratic, original, attractive and successful 18th- and early-19th-century domestic town architecture is to be found in the seaside and spa resorts that grew up in this period.

The Royal Crescent, Bath

THE SPA TOWN
Architectural Good Health

Of all resort towns, Bath was the earliest and best. It was precocious in many ways – not least architecturally – and most other spa towns were late in developing into fully-fledged resorts. The health-giving qualities of spa waters had been recognized for centuries; in one move developers in spa towns provided both the requisite accommodation and the architectural backdrop, as the boundaries between health, leisure and the pursuit of fashion became increasingly blurred. We might think of the architecture of the spa town as a kind of medicinal aesthetics, contributing to a general feeling of wellbeing, despite the gripes of John Gwynn, Mrs Montagu, Smollett's Squire Bramble and others about Bath.

OPPOSITE:

Superimposed orders of columns at The Circus, Bath, were a significant but well-advised investment of design effort and money in a speculative development.

The Woods and Bath

No one did more for the architecture of Bath (and, by example, for that of many other towns and cities) than John Wood the Elder (1704–54). The son of a builder, Wood worked in London before returning to his hometown in 1727, at the age of 23. He soon established himself as the city's leading architect, and set about doing for Bath's appearance what the infamous Regency dandy Beau Nash had done for its manners. By the time of his death, Wood had, with boldness and perspicacity, bought up and planned the ambitious development of a large residential area beyond the city walls, thereby bypassing the restrictions the city's corporation had placed on building within the city itself. Wood had also articulated the historical and aesthetic drive behind his plans in his *Essay towards a Description of Bath* (1742-3), in which he carefully enunciated how he had improved the standard of accommodation in the city, painting a picture of 'before' and 'after' which left no reader in doubt as to his central role in the city's improvement. The tone of the book is immodest, but Wood was claiming no more than his due. His son, also named John, took over the project after his father's death.

Wood senior's chief innovation, as we have seen, was the palace front applied to a terrace of houses (see page 60). He was not the first to think of this, but its appearance at Queen Square, a development that was constructed from 1729, was the first truly urban expression of this solution to the problem of how to 'wrap' a row of houses. The quality wrapping might have led onlookers to think that the contents had a matching sophistication and grandeur, but that was its role. The onlooker might have been disappointed, but he or she benefited none the less from the veneer of gentility that palatial finishes provided for all. Wood himself described the north side of Queen Square as '[soaring] above the other buildings with a sprightliness which gives it the elegance and grandeur of the body of a stately Palace'. Not everyone was disappointed with the discrepancy between Bath's exteriors and interiors. Jane Austen, lodging in Queen Square in 1799, was 'exceedingly pleased with the house', and found the rooms 'quite as large as we expected'.

Through no fault of his own, outcome fell short of ambition at Wood's North and South Parades, but Wood may have deliberately contrived the contrast between the

ABOVE: *John Wood the Elder's Queen Square, Bath, pulls off the 'palace front' trick much better than most. The façades read initially as one grand unit, as the columns and pediment divert attention from the ground floor, where the individual doorways give the game away.*

palatial and distinctive architecture of Queen Square, the Circus and Royal Crescent and the fairly standard houses in between. The lower-order houses gain much from their role within the complex as a whole. Despite the proximity of delightful hilly countryside, the view from the Bath town house (like that in London's better developments) largely comprised the town's domestic architecture itself. Another town house was the chief object

of contemplation from the windows of the town house. Nowhere was this truer than at the Circus in Bath: a long time in the planning and making, but popular from its outset. The Circus also formed the archetypal example of the individual town house sacrificed to the interests of the greater whole. The rotunda may be a splendid thing by which to be visually and physically embraced, but its shape inevitably leads to wedge-shaped rooms

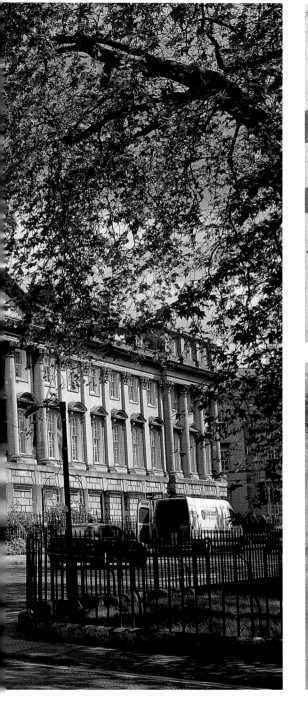

that could never be seen as 'convenient'.

The Royal Crescent, which was completed in the 1770s, was the culmination of Wood's planned ceremonial route through his new Bath. Here both terrace and houses were at their grandest. Bath's Royal Crescent played a different game of reciprocity between house and viewer: its elevated position and shallow curve meant that it was less engaged with itself and its neighbours, and instead looked out onto both country and city at some distance. At the same time it provided an object to be appreciated from that distance as well as by those promenading close by.

We have a tendency today to consider all rows of splendid Georgian houses as permanently at their social peak, and only perhaps latterly fallen on bad times, if at all. But even the Royal Crescent was not consistently prestigious. It may have justified its royal tag when the Duke and Duchess of

ABOVE AND BELOW:

Bath stone worked to good effect in details from Great Pulteney Street and the Circus, in Bath. The attention that John Wood paid to ornamenting the metopes here with a range of emblematic motifs was typical only of John Wood.

ABOVE AND LEFT:
The Study and Drawing Room at No 1 Royal Crescent, Bath, recreate generic high-quality Georgian interiors. Shallow mouldings painted in a contrasting colour create 'panels' which break up expanses of plain wall. Likewise, the 'compartmented' carpets subdivide the floorspace into central and border zones.

York entertained the Prince of Wales there in 1796, but by the 19th century the Royal Crescent's houses were divided into lodgings, suggesting a considerable decline in status. Of course there was always the danger that a house could make itself susceptible to such division simply by virtue of being larger than average.

Unlike John Nash's stucco expanses at Regent's Park (see pages 104–107), which were planned almost a century after John Wood's Bath, the best architecture is designed to be appreciated in passing and lingered on at leisure. The new Bath provided delights and contrasts at every turn, and maintained a consistent quality of design and finish, greatly helped by the use of Bath stone, as well as by the Woods' personal oversight of the city's most prominent domestic features. As other speculators helped Bath's expansion along, every conceivable architectural device for articulating a terrace or cres-

cent was employed, making the city the showcase of Georgian urban domestic architecture that it remains to this day. Wood the Elder had brought the Picturesque to Bath almost a century before it had a serious impact on town planning elsewhere. But in the late 18th century, Thomas Baldwin (1750–1820), who was Bath's designated architect from 1780, demonstrated the impact that neo-classical restraint could have in the right hands and on the right scale. The shallow decoration at Great Pulteney Street is sufficient to enhance its excessive length (1,000 feet/300 metres) and width (100 feet/30 metres), but not enough to overwhelm it.

Buxton

Bath benefited from the Woods' artistic and speculative ambitions, their control and their importation of skilled craftsmen; from the use of Bath stone; and from the

ABOVE: *John Carr's Crescent at Buxton revisited Inigo Jones's Covent Garden after a gap of almost 150 years, catering for the needs of residence, leisure and commerce with shops, lodgings, and two hotels.*

ABOVE: The colonnade at Buxton's Crescent provides space for promenading, shelter and business.

the Tudor Earls of Leicester and Warwick, but it was the fifth Duke of Devonshire, William Cavendish (1748–1811), who set about rivalling Bath commercially and architecturally from around 1779; his architect was the talented John Carr of York (1723–1807). Buxton's semicircular Crescent, which started things off and remained the principal feature of the town, cannot rival the Royal Crescent at Bath, which was completed only a few years beforehand. Nevertheless, it is undeniably stylish in a more understated way. Its lengthy façade, which stretches 360 feet (110 metres), is articulated by giant Doric pilasters standing over an arcaded ground floor containing shops. In its provision of a mixture of lodgings, hotels and commercial premises, as well as in its façade composition, the Crescent at Buxton is strongly reminiscent of Inigo Jones's Covent Garden piazza (see pages 25-28). At the same time, it is a visually pared down but physically extended version of Robert Adam's front to 20 St James's Square, London, erected just a few years before (see page 62). The repetition of Adam's façade on the adjacent house in St James's Square detracted from its almost perfect expression of the nature of the individual town-house front. But at Buxton, the essence of Adam's façade divisions and ornament proved perfectly extendable to a lengthy front, with no differentiation between houses at all. A comparison of the two developments – 20 St James's Square and the Crescent – shows how effective variations on the town-house formula of a rusticated, (real or blind) arcaded ground floor, giant pilasters, entablature and cornice, and balustrade could be in both circumstances.

A Mania for Bricks and Mortar

Cheltenham has a long history as a town, but it only grew up as a fashionable resort between the late 1780s and the 1820s, and by the 1840s its glory days were over. The medicinal springs were discovered in 1716, and piecemeal developments related the site

conventions of 18th-century architecture. Other towns fared less well. They were successful and impressive in parts, but never matched Bath, which proved itself the model Georgian city. Most other successful spa towns developed considerably later than Bath – from the 1770s – even if their waters were discovered and tapped much earlier than that. Buxton's waters were known to the Romans, as evidenced by baths lying beneath the town's Crescent and the present spa buildings. Illustrious visitors included Mary Queen of Scots and

of the first well to other urban features, including newly erected assembly rooms and a theatre. Although in 1786 an Act of Parliament legislated for the town's improvement, including better paving and lighting, it was an extended holiday taken by George III and his family at Lord Fauconberg's house in 1788 that ensured that Cheltenham became firmly fashionable.

Other wells developed and the town's population grew rapidly, from 3,000 at the turn of the century to 20,000 in 1826, not including seasonal visitors. Just as construction activity in London in the 1760s was described as a 'rage of building', so Cheltenham's rapid development in the 1820s was termed a 'brick and mortar mania'. The 'mania' attracted entrepreneurs and development land exchanged hands for considerable sums of money. The Lansdown Estate was purchased early on by London financier Henry Thompson, whose son commissioned architect J. B. Papworth (1775–1847) to prepare a suitable plan for the estate on the theme of *rus in urbe* (the country in the town). Cheltenham was specifically a summer resort, and it generally adopted a less urban aspect in the setting of its buildings than Bath. The result was England's first provincial garden suburb, with both terraces and individual houses set among avenues and gardens, somewhat in the manner of John Nash's work at Regent's Park in London (see pages 104-107). Lansdown Place was built as planned, but a banking crisis in 1825 put paid to Papworth's planned layouts of Lansdown Terrace and Lansdown Crescent, which were only partly adhered to. Papworth found himself and his plans ousted when Robert and Charles Jearrad took over from Thompson junior in 1830. Nevertheless, the result remained an elegant manifestation of the best that sub-Greek Revival architecture had to offer, in an attractively leafy setting. Even the Jearrad buildings display 'economy without meanness', with stucco or stone fronts and cast iron balconies. The same principal was at work inside the houses, 'with simple marble

fireplaces, mahogany door surrounds, and plaster friezes of fruit and foliage'.

Of the Lansdown Estate houses themselves, those in the Parade (c. 1835–38) took a distinct step away from the classic town house; they were only two-storey structures, and were weighted heavily at the bottom by tallish Doric pedimented porches. Occasional pediments along the roofline paid homage to earlier 'palace fronts', but the stylish, heavy porches ensured that nothing else of the illusion remained. Lansdown Crescent, finished at

ABOVE: Excellent cast-iron balconies attached to the ashlar face of Lansdown Place, Cheltenham, make early use of the ubiquitous double-heart motif.

ABOVE: *Bulky Doric porches fronting houses of fairly squat proportions at Lansdown Parade, Cheltenham, herald the demise of the verticality and flatness of later 18th- and earlier 19th-century facades. This terrace from c.1835-8 looks more like a series of suburban villas incidentally and rather reluctantly attached to each other.*

balcony laid the uniformity of the town-house terrace open to disruption, while also allowing some degree of response to the individual house itself.

Finally, Lansdown Terrace, completed in 1834, showed houses marked out as individuals, but at the same time incorporated in a terrace. The terrace itself had no pretensions to form a palace front, but the houses themselves did, in a distinctly odd way. Papworth would not have tolerated such heavy handling of a façade or a row, but these houses nevertheless demonstrated a further, if idiosyncratic, approach to the town-house façade, with one side of each house given an oddly wide pedimented balcony at first-floor level, which gave that side the appearance of being the whole house, while the other side sat quietly by, as not participating in the town-house aesthetic.

Leamington

Like Cheltenham, Leamington developed as a spa town from humbler roots in the late 18th century. It reached its peak both socially and architecturally in the 1800s, particularly the 1820s to 1840s. The tags 'Royal' and 'Spa' were added in 1838 with Queen Victoria's blessing. Leamington largely escaped the heftiness of much terrace-based town-house architecture of this period. Even the Ionic porticoes at Waterloo Place were not sufficient to counteract the impact of the restraint of the rest of the building, and their bulk was, in any case, alleviated by elegant neo-classical ironwork running the entire length of the terrace. Lansdowne Crescent dismissed porticoes in favour of elegant ironwork verandas, finished with a linearity that complemented the classic town-house-ness of the buildings behind. The same style was carried over to Lansdowne Circus, where it proved equally well suited to semi-detached houses. As with other 19th-century villas, these elegant homes retained the air of the classic town house aesthetic by tucking their doors to the side in an extra, narrow bay.

much the same time, did better, with the Jearrads' restraint paying off with a very long but none the less unified front, articulated by little more than its paired Doric porches and simple balconies. However, the four storeys made all the difference.

Lansdown Place moved in yet another direction, blurring the distinction between terraced town house and semi-detached villa. The houses were tall, with half basements and attics either side of their three main storeys, of which the central one (a lofty first floor) carried a cast-iron balcony. But the houses were paired, and each pair linked by recessed porch, marking a distinct move from the unity of the terrace, even if much of the town-house aesthetic remained. The inconsistency at first-floor level showed how the applied

ABOVE: *The shallow Lansdowne Crescent, Leamington, relies largely on ironwork to ornament and bind the houses together.*

RIGHT: *At Lansdowne Circus, Leamington, the terrace has started unravelling into pairs of villas, even if the houses still cling to the town-house aesthetic.*

THE SEASIDE TOWN

A Room With a View

The publication of Dr Russell's *Dissertation Concerning the Uses of Sea Water in Diseases of the Glands*, published in Latin in 1750 and in English in 1753, brought the benefits of bathing in the sea to public attention. The response was soon evident architecturally, especially toward the end of the 18th century, as a number of squares, crescents and terraces were built in such places as Brighton, Weymouth, Southend and Bognor, as well as in Margate, whose Cecil Square, which was laid out in 1769, seems to have initiated the architectural development of seaside resorts.

Such seaside developments provided accommodation – generally short-term lodgings – for visitors of all but the lowest classes. They often also offered scope for large-scale town planning on virgin land, with natural features – a bay, a cliff, or simply a sea view – ripe for architectural exploitation. It might seem extraordinary to a present-day public that values a marine prospect so highly that as late as 1772 Weymouth was the first seaside development to turn to the sea, with the building of the Royal Hotel. The earlier squares and streets catering for sea-bathers at Margate were laid out north of the old village and a little inland from the coast and harbour. John Newman has suggested that the first users of the bathing machine, which was invented by a local Quaker in 1753, 'preferred, characteristically, not to overlook the sea when they were not actually in it'. At Weymouth, the terraces erected from the 1770s, although built in different phases by different builders, formed a crescent that swept around the bay, and the classical idiom they shared provided a kind of default harmony and homogeneity where none was necessarily contrived. In its western extremes especially, the bay also provided the space from which to view the buildings – an important element in the

systematic grouping of town houses. But aesthetic appreciation need not take place on solid ground. Just as the sea could be admired from houses, so the houses could be admired from the sea, either by boat or, more probably, by a stroll along a lengthy pier, for example the Chain Pier, Brighton. In a similar feat of reciprocity, the Adam brothers' Royal Terrace at the Adelphi (from 1768) not only offered views over the Thames, but was designed to be viewed from the river itself, which experienced much heavier traffic then than it does now, as well as from the opposite bank (see page 68).

The earliest, the biggest and the best of seaside architectural schemes can still be found in and around Brighton. The town's history as a resort begins with Dr Russell's *Dissertation* and the neat coincidence of his discovery of an iron-rich chalybeate spring in St Ann's Well Garden. Both sea and spa attracted genteel visitors, and, from the 1760s, royalty: the Duke of Gloucester; the Duke of Cumberland; and, most famously, the Prince of Wales (later George IV), who came to Brighton in 1783, 1785 and 1786. Like other seaside houses, the Marine Pavilion, designed by Henry Holland (1745–1806) and built for the Prince of Wales in 1786–87, kept its distance from the sea. But the first of Brighton's great, unified architectural compositions – the Royal Crescent – turned to acknowledge the sea and beach from 1798. Development took off and surpassed even Bath in its scale. Much of what we think of as quintessentially Brighton dates from the 1820s and 1830s, even if the later arrival of the railway made it more accessible than ever to greater numbers of visitors.

ABOVE: *The three-bay town-house front puffs itself out with a profusion of Regency bows at Brunswick Square, Brighton.*

OPPOSITE: *Curves add grandeur to both greater and lesser terraces at Brighton. Whether understated in brick or overstated in stucco, the terrace became the accepted means of creating or expanding an urban development.*

BALCONIES AND VERANDAHS

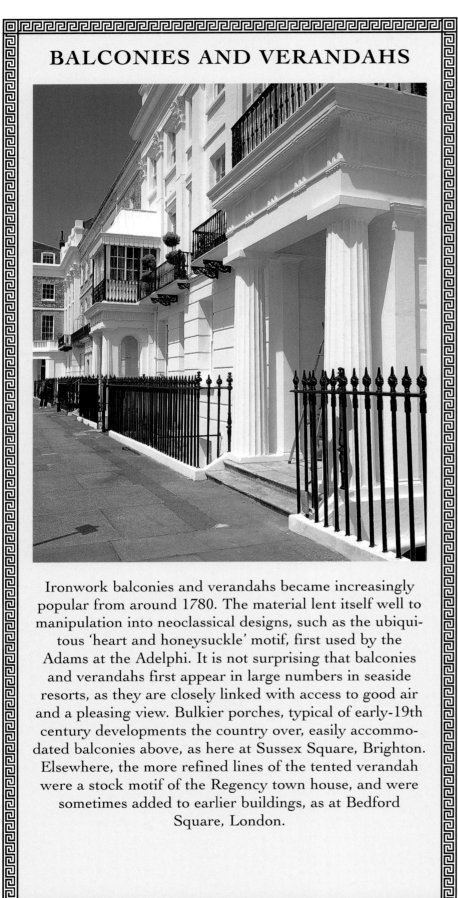

Ironwork balconies and verandahs became increasingly popular from around 1780. The material lent itself well to manipulation into neoclassical designs, such as the ubiquitous 'heart and honeysuckle' motif, first used by the Adams at the Adelphi. It is not surprising that balconies and verandahs first appear in large numbers in seaside resorts, as they are closely linked with access to good air and a pleasing view. Bulkier porches, typical of early-19th century developments the country over, easily accommodated balconies above, as here at Sussex Square, Brighton. Elsewhere, the more refined lines of the tented verandah were a stock motif of the Regency town house, and were sometimes added to earlier buildings, as at Bedford Square, London.

Brunswick Square and Terrace form a composition dating from 1825–27, and show a very distinct debt to John Nash's work at Regent's Park, London (see pages 104-107).

The two rows comprising Brunswick Terrace are each of 39 bays, successfully articulated by giant pilasters and strong accents. Brunswick Square is generously sized, although still smaller than Kemp Town's Lewes Crescent or Sussex Square. Here the articulation is less coherent, with shallow bows stretching across house fronts, some with an Ionic order, some without. The later north side has giant pilasters but no accent. The scheme is impressive, but by no means perfect. The same architects began construction in Kemp Town in 1823. Thomas Cubitt (1788–1856), better known for his work in London, was commissioned to build houses in Lewes Crescent. Like the Brunswick Square development, Kemp Town looks to Regent's Park, but loses something of the London scheme's flair in the translation. The excessive size of both the Crescent and Sussex Square make their façades difficult to read as compositions, but they do little beyond accenting in giant pilasters in any case. Like other seaside towns, Brighton demonstrates bold ambition tempered with a relaxed air appropriate to the seaside but detrimental to its architecture. None the less, this is the home of the seaside town house par excellence – stucco, pilasters and columns, pretty iron balconies, verandahs and an abundance of bays and bows.

Sidmouth

This same seaside licence is also found at Sidmouth in Devon, although it takes a very different form. Better known for its real specialty – the cottage orné – Sidmouth is an idiosyncratic gem in the history of the town house. Its development from a small fishing town into a popular bathing resort began at the end of the 18th century. Its architectural development soon followed, with a London developer

and theatre designer, Michael Novosielski (1750–95), designing the stuccoed Fortfield Terrace as a speculative venture for the lord of the manor in 1792. It was an impressive start for what is still a relatively small resort, but Novosielski's death three years later meant the terrace was never finished to his designs. The building phases are apparent, and they dissipate Sidmouth's intended grandeur, demonstrating again how precarious the business of the palace front was, and how its ambitions could not be achieved through half measures. The shallow crescent overlooking the sea, but at some distance from the shore, is attractive none the less, and certainly outshines later, shorter terraces. But it is elsewhere, on a smaller scale, and with more informality, that Sidmouth's special nature really shines through.

As we will see when looking at John Nash's development at Regent's Park in the next chapter, the town house generally played its role in the Picturesque movement of the late 18th and early 19th centuries when grouped with others and placed artfully in a landscaped setting. But at Sidmouth, individual houses demonstrated something of the Picturesque through their own devices. The arrangement of openings in the façade was sufficiently asymmetrical to look Picturesque, yet not so far off the mark as to lose all connection with the classic house from which it derived. In addition, and as something of an excuse for the mild asymmetry, the openings were Gothicized, with pointed arches and marginal glazing. Within this general Gothic scheme the standard elements of early 19th-century seaside

ABOVE RIGHT AND LEFT: *Fine neoclassical detail is the icing on the cake at 13 Brunswick Square, Brighton, now the Regency Town House Museum.*

ABOVE: Beach House, Sidmouth, goes its own way with an appropriately Picturesque, asymmetric arrangement of Regency Gothick windows and cast-iron balconies, between loosely classical end pilasters.

bathers from before 1730. The playwright Richard Brinsley Sheridan wrote his *Trip to Scarborough* in 1777. The better architectural elements came later, developing from the 1830s. Like other towns, Scarborough was reluctant to turn to the sea. Its principal architectural feat, something of a match for Bath, was the Crescent (*c.* 1830–32), which comprised two ashlar-faced terraces of four-storey houses that faced the inland valley. The Crescent's lengthy façades were relieved by cast-iron balconies on the first floor and terminated by six-bay angle pavilions with giant pilasters. But the town was too remote from most of the country, at least before the arrival of the railway, to be popular with anything but northern aristocracy and gentry, and much of its housing is both later and smaller in scale.

Whitby's development as a seaside resort also came with the railway's arrival in 1847, although the town's better 18th-century houses reflect the prosperity it first achieved from whaling and from shipping alum, which was mined nearby. In 1848, the railway king George Hudson purchased West Cliff Fields and began a development scheme, later taken over by Sir George Elliot. Perhaps its late start as a resort is why Whitby never rivalled the likes of Brighton in its architecture. Even its High Victorian buildings represent nothing better than underachievement. Whitby's Crescent had promise, but was only half built. The town's houses are undistinguished, showing what could happen, aesthetically, when group effort collapsed and the individual house was left, unexpectedly, to its own resources.

architecture were placed – bow windows and tented balconies.

Scarborough and Whitby

A spa resort that was comparable in its development to Bath was Scarborough. Mineral springs were discovered on its beach around 1620. By the end of the 17th century the springs were being visited by 'people of good fashion', who walked or drove on the sands, and they continued to grow in popularity to the end of the 18th century. Unlike Bath, Scarborough also offered the delights of the sea, attracting

ABOVE: *Houses at St Hilda's Terrace, Whitby, from the late 1770s, display little imagination in continuing to exploit the potential for a central pedimented section in imitation of a smallish country house of forty years earlier.*

RIGHT: *An attractive roof lantern lets in light at 19 Grape Lane, Whitby.*

CONCLUSION

Capitalizing on Space

In spa and seaside towns we find a scale of development matched in few other places, with more or less design control exercised over individual terraces, squares and crescents. Because this 'mania' related to new buildings rather than refurbishments, the identity of the single town house was generally only expressed negatively, where the parts of a terrace failed to match, rather than through a positive decision to be different.

As in London and other major cities, construction of terraces was often piecemeal; but the topography of the seaside town in particular often allowed terraces to be viewed at some distance, and their lapses were therefore more evident. But the space in seaside towns allowed for bigger, detached houses, and, as in many other provincial towns over the centuries, these were where individuality was expressed. Most importantly, the terrace and its variations in the resort town was used to make something of a location; it was a starting point in itself, not infilling or expansion at a town's edges. As such, while still driven by the capitalist interests of estate development and the economics of speculative building, the architecture of the resort towns generally had greater potential for a combination of grandeur and exuberance than was often the case elsewhere. The unity of these developments also means that they have suffered least from the ravages of 20th-century demolition, and remain in place as eloquent spokesmen for an elegant period.

LEFT: A criss-cross pattern of vertical and horizontal emphasis at East Cliff House, Ramsgate, achieving a surprisingly successful balance of diverse architectural features.

OPPOSITE: The extensive terrace at Waterloo Place, Leamington, softens projecting Ionic porches with delicate ironwork balconies to create a satisfying pattern along an otherwise plain façade.

CHAPTER FOUR

VICTORIAN VARIETY

The Nineteenth-century Town House

When we think of Victorian houses, we tend to conjure up an image of a few great country houses and rows of middle-class and working-class terraces. We also think of suburbia. But what happened to the town house proper in this era? Although this story is moving into the 19th century, it is, to start with, a continuation of the 18th-century story. In London, a distinct change in style did not emerge until later in the century, and other towns developing in this period, particularly in the north of England, were still catching up with what London and Bath had achieved in the 18th century and early in the 19th century. After all, the Victorian age didn't begin until 1837. But although the changes were often subtle in the earlier part of the 19th century, they were none the less significant in this account of the classic English town house. What is more, something very new was lurking around the corner, which was set to disrupt the Georgian aesthetic of the town house altogether.

Nos 5-10 Belgrave Square, London

THE GEORGIAN LEGACY

More of the Same

As Benjamin Disraeli observed, 18th-century town houses already lined street upon street, with some degree of monotony, particularly in London:

your ... Baker Streets and Harley Streets, and Wimpole Streets, and all those flat, dull, spiritless streets, all [resemble] each other, like a large family of plain children, with Portland Place and Portman Square for their respectable parents.
Tancred, 1847

Certainly Victorian London looked, for some while, little different to Georgian London, and it was not until later in the century that the distinctly Victorian town house appeared at either the upper or lower ends of the market. And the former never emerged in the numbers that the Georgian town house did, mainly because growth was necessarily away from the city centre. Disraeli voiced the general Victorian dislike of the Georgian terrace, but there was no impetus to change within the confines of the town itself. As he noted, the stock was already there, and it did not yet need replacing.

John Nash and Regent's Park
Even if classicism remained the language of urban domestic development, the ways in which that classical language was handled

OPPOSITE: *Like the rest of Regent's Park, Gloucester Gate pulls out all the stops, with palace-front articulation, columns, pediments and stucco.*

LEFT: *New fashion reflected in fine ironwork rather than the house front itself, at Lansdowne Crescent, Leamington.*

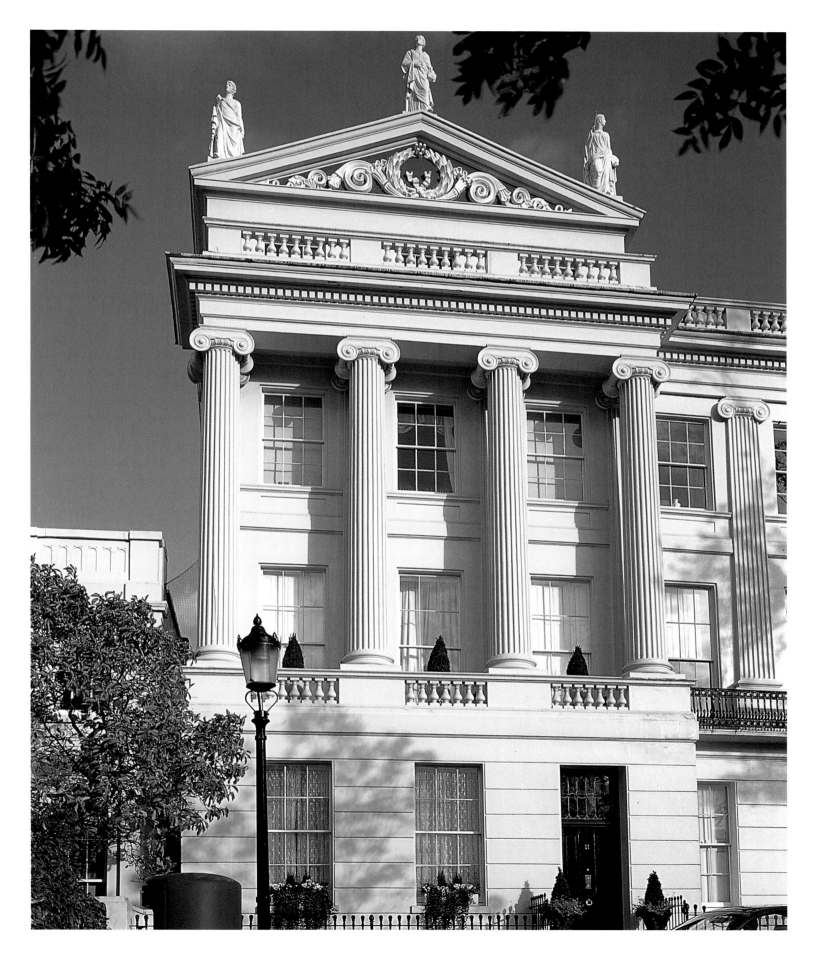

Fig. 5.

Fig. 1.

Fig. 2.

Fig. 3.

did develop in the 19th century. We can go no further in this story without describing and discussing the terraces at Regent's Park, which were designed by John Nash (1752–1835) from 1812. This project was such that the needs of picturesque urban landscaping necessitated a variety of approaches within and between terraces. Regent's Park was London's major development of the first half of the century, and set a benchmark for all English towns with any aspirations to grandeur in their domestic architecture. We have already seen Regent's Park used as a model at the seaside and the spa town (see pages 89 & 96), and we will soon see how it leads the way, and is sometimes surpassed, in other provincial towns and cities.

Nash's work at Regent's Park shows well how the town house often responded to changing fashions and aesthetic movements, using its group identity rather than the individual appearance of each residence. That was part of the charm of the town house for builders and buyers alike, especially within major conurbations. The town house could be bang up to date, even when the way it looked was just a slight advance on how it had looked 50 years earlier. Summerson describes Regent's Park as 'a fascinating interplay of Picturesque aesthetics and economic expediency'. Nash's greatest contribution to urban domestic architecture – and the reason why this part of the classical story must appear in this chapter – was that he did not perpetuate the 18th-century tendency for grids of streets and squares. Instead, he put the newly explored aesthetic of the Picturesque to good use, creating a scheme that was at once grander and more humane. In Nash's townscape, accommodation and environment are not merely complementary, but well and truly integrated.

Nash was no genius when it came to the smaller details of design, but that hardly mattered given his inventiveness in creating an urban plan on an unheard-of scale, which took landscaping as its starting point and then provided the requisite buildings in that context. The overall design concept came well before the architectural character of its constituent parts. Nash's ability to adopt, often with little true precision or understanding, any number of classical expressions came into its own here, with constant shifts of style and pace within and between buildings and every concession to the viewer. The individual town house is subjugated to the greater good – but what or who would not wish to be part of this grander scheme of things? The finish on the buildings may have lacked finesse in both design and execution, but Nash had raised the stakes and showed how to make the palace front *truly* resemble a palace, in a palace setting, at least from a distance.

In Nash's scheme it is evident that more attention has been paid to external appearance, not just in terms of the Picturesque feel of the overall scheme, but within the individual terraces themselves. This occurs more and more as the century goes on and turns its back on the rectitude of the early Georgian terrace in ever stranger, non-classical ways. At this point, though, Nash's means of articulating a terrace façade was just a more powerful version of what had gone before – extra-strong emphasis in the centre and at the ends, with a degree of movement and massiveness alien to the lighter touch of the late 18th-century architects, at least in this field. In their monumentality, Nash's terraces owed almost as much to the Sublime as to the Picturesque.

A combination of wealth and cheaper materials may account for the increased decoration on the front of terraces after about 1815, but it was also the result, no doubt, of an aesthetic desire for more variety between palace fronts, as they were so common by this point. For the same reason, developers needed to provide their

rows with marks of distinction. Just as in the 18th century, however, criticism followed sharply on the heels of stylistic innovation. As the historian Dr Stefan Muthesius points out:

Nash had already censured recent developments on the Portland Estate for bad workmanship hidden behind lavish façades, a criticism soon to be levelled against his own work. The article in the Surveyor, Engineer and Architect *of 1841 used the most vitriolic language against Nash and others. 'Trumpery' became a fashionable word.*

ABOVE: *C. A. Busby's design for a house at Brunswick Terrace, Brighton, c.1825, builds on the 'vertical' aesthetic perfected by Robert Adam, George Dance and others in the preceding decades.*

OPPOSITE: *Plans for a 'first rate' house from* The New and Improved Practical Builder, *1856.*

THE TRAPPINGS OF SUCCESS

Colonizing the Industrial Town

Beyond London, many towns and cities were subject to great changes in their domestic architecture in the later part of the 18th century and the early part of the 19th century, as they followed and sometimes surpassed the capital's lead. We have already seen how spa and seaside towns responded swiftly and often effectively to the example set by Nash at Regent's Park (see pages 104-107). Although seaside architecture in particular had its own idiosyncrasies – not least a profusion of bay windows to admit light and a view – shared Picturesque aims led to comparable solutions, which put the sheer bulk of new building stock and the free-for-all on classical ornamentation to good effect in both places.

BELOW: *Reticent house fronts make their contribution to the overall scheme of things at Clayton Street, Newcastle.*

Industrial towns and the major ports had rather different aims. Here, in accommodating a swiftly expanding population, the objective was not always, or simply, to exploit a view or the natural topography, but rather to express civic, mercantile or industrial success. While most of the towns that burgeoned in this period had long and sometimes glorious histories – and their own share of 18th-century houses – their rapid and more planned physical expansion at this time offered scope for townscaping, the results of which soon outshone the more piecemeal or reticent expressions of classical domestic architecture in the previous century. The success of these towns brought with it not only larger numbers of people, but also different types of resident requiring accommodation, particularly among the wealthy middle classes. This was not the period of the affluent townsman or local estate owner expressing his own success and merit in an individual classicizing front, as was so often witnessed in the 18th-century provincial town, but an era of the town itself making a proud and fitting display.

In both cases, however, the medium of expression was the classically styled town house, on its own or in bulk.

The Town House in the North

Newcastle distinguished itself from other industrial northern towns that burgeoned in the early 19th century with the style and quality of its townscaping and architecture, as planned by developer Richard Grainger (1797–1861). By this point, Newcastle had been a major coal-exporting port for two centuries, and was home to several impressive houses from the 17th and 18th centuries to prove it. In 1698 the traveller Celia Fiennes reported that '[Newcastle] most resembles London of any place in England, its buildings lofty and large of brick mostly or stone, the streetes very broad and handsome'. In the 18th century, the city's forward-thinking Corporation laid out new streets to ease traffic congestion, and streets and squares of new brick houses were erected. The town's first formal square was Charlotte Square (although construction on Hanover Square began in 1720, it was never completed), and together with the new Assembly Rooms built nearby, it indicated 'a growing social and architectural sophistication'. Newcastle benefited from the input of a series of good architects even before Grainger came on the scene in about 1820 to provide further impetus to the developments started 50 years earlier.

Although Grainger started off in brick at Higham Place (1819–20), he soon expressed the ambitions of both himself and the town in the extensive and skilful use of regularized pieces of masonry, which characterized early 19th-century Newcastle. Eldon Square (1825–31) and Leazes Terrace (1829–34) were the first physical signs of this ambition, and the

BELOW: All that remains of one of Richard Grainger's earliest schemes in Newcastle, Eldon Square. High-quality ashlar facing, executed in a simple Greek style, and ironwork balconies banding the row together, result in an appropriately domestic monumentality.

Leazes development in particular, which was designed by Thomas Oliver, beat Nash at his own game by finishing in stone rather than stucco. What's more, the square was enviably spacious, with 86 bays to the east and 21 to the west. Even if they followed the capital's lead in many respects, the provinces were certainly not its poor relations in terms of the quality of their domestic architecture. Here, the impact was achieved not only through size, but also through a standard of quality and a restraint of external finish that could have taught contemporary London and its seaside imitators a lesson.

By 1834 Newcastle's Corporation had accepted Grainger's proposal for a new centre combining commercial and domestic accommodation. Five years later, Grainger had erected Grey Street, Grainger Street and Clayton Street, among others. The historian Nikolaus Pevsner (1902–83) described the architecture as 'competent and resourceful in the varying of the limited number of elements with which a classical architect could operate, and convincing in its appearance of solidity'. In addition, Grainger was able to exploit both the dramatic potential of the slope to the river and the earlier townscape, to prevent his development falling into the trap of monotony.

Liverpool's development goes back to the Middle Ages, although serious growth began in the 17th century. The population increased at an astonishing rate, rising from around 6,000 in the 17th century to nearly 80,000 in 1801. By 1821 the number was close to 120,000; 20 years later it had more than doubled again. Earlier trade with the Americas and the West Indies was in sugar, tobacco and cotton, but the much less reputable slave trade was added to Liverpool's portfolio in the early 18th century, and accounted for much of the city's wealth as the century wore on. Celia Fiennes was impressed by Liverpool too, describing the town as

ABOVE: *Ashlar-faced grandeur and a giant Ionic order on this seven-bay façade set the pace at Gambier Terrace, Liverpool, in the 1830s. Unfortunately, the composition was not completed to plan.*

'London in miniature', and writing of houses 'high and even' and inhabitants 'very well dressed and of good fashion'. But Liverpool's star truly rose in the 19th century, when it settled into its role as England's prime Atlantic port, with passengers added to the types of cargo from the 1840s. The town expressed its greatly increased population and its mercantile success in architectural developments, particularly in the 1830s, carrying on where earlier developments such as Rodney Street had left off.

Like Newcastle, 18th-century Liverpool was built in brick, but the more ambitious developers of the 19th century often looked to stone to provide adequate expression to the town's self-satisfaction. At Percy and Huskisson Streets, Falkner Square and the west side of Gambier Terrace, stucco, stone and columns aggrandize the building stock. The reservations voiced by the 18th-century critics regarding external decoration appropriate to a person's class had no place here. In any event, such principles had already been abandoned in London, and there was certainly no impetus to pay them any heed in a town where wealth was almost wholly derived from commercial or mercantile activity. In fact, in this context the appropriation of the trappings of 'palatial' architecture was a real expression of the rise of the wealthy middle classes in this era, even if this was not consciously intended. Things were exactly the way the reactionary Georgian gentleman had feared they would be – and the upset was being expressed through the town house above all.

Bristol's Buildings

Splendid new developments were not the prerogative of the northern cities. In the south-west, Bristol followed a similar pattern to Liverpool. A flurry of building activity at Clifton in the closing years of the 18th century actually began as part of an attempt to establish Hotwells as a spa along the architectural lines of nearby Bath, but continued as a means of catering for Bristol's growing population, which had reached nearly 70,000 by 1801, rivalling its northern counterpart. As discussed earlier, Bristol's sources of wealth were similar to those of Liverpool, most particularly with regard to the slave trade (see page 60). One of the earlier Clifton terraces – Pevsner calls it the 'most presumptuous' – was Windsor Terrace (c. 1790–1810). It was intended to be

stone fronted, but in the end only two houses got the full treatment while the remainder were rendered, so that its unending march of fluted Corinthian giant pilasters is not enough to make it as grand as it would like to think itself. In the true spirit of 'façadism', there are sometimes three rather than two storeys stuffed in behind the giant pilasters. The better Clifton architecture emerged in the 1810s to 1840s, including the remarkably long Royal York Crescent (c. 1810–20), with over 130 bays, but plain doorways, first-floor verandahs and none of the pretensions of its predecessor. Terraces in the Grecian style proved to be Clifton's specialty, including Worcester Terrace, which was completed as late as the mid-1850s and was proof of the remarkably long and healthy survival of the classical English

ABOVE LEFT: Brick terraces of the 1830s-40s at Huskisson Street, Liverpool, are relieved from monotony by Ionic porches.

ABOVE RIGHT: A detail from one of Bristol's most impressive groups of houses, at Prince Street, from the 1720s. No 66, shown here, is distinguished from its neighbours by a central feature of giant fluted pilasters supporting a segmental pediment.

terrace house. Worcester Terrace was also a demonstration of how the external finish kept pace with changing fashions within the classical idiom – from Artisan Mannerism, to Baroque, to Palladian, to Neoclassical, to Greek – while the house itself changed little at all.

Classicism spread not only by observation of built examples, but through publications. Pattern-books, manuals and price books continued to thrive, although they were soon replaced by new types of publication, notably the trade catalogue and the architectural magazine. As in the 18th century, pattern-books paid little attention to terraced houses. It was not until 1837 that a pattern-book was primarily devoted to this subject: J. Collis's *Builders' Portfolio of Street Architecture* contained 19 neoclassical designs for façades of houses and other buildings. The façades of the first-rate houses carry on where the later 18th-century designers left off, with a flat, pilastered look that was well suited to the town house, if a little old-fashioned by this time. On the whole, as we have seen, experimentation was increasingly likely to be on the scale of a row rather than an individual street house. And it was even more likely to be focused, both in the pub-

lications and in practice, on the suburban villa, which proved to be the true home of the affluent middle classes as the 19th century proceeded. The town house's rival for architectural attention was no longer the country house – which it could never hope to beat – but the detached or semi-detached home, which lent itself more readily to the kind of experimentation with style that characterized the middle and later parts of the 19th century, as we will soon see. Nevertheless, there were elements of the terraced house which allowed it to accommodate variety as long as any style play was limited to the façade.

PLAYING WITH STYLE

The Town House Dresses Up

BELOW: *Milner Square, London, strikes a happy balance between verticality and horizontality, offering a refreshing take on neoclassical elegance and restraint with a surprisingly modern air for the 1840s.*

The clear distinction between the 'standard' terraced house façade and what lay behind troubled many critics, as we have seen. But it was part of the charm and appeal of the classic town house that its often blank, expressionless façade disguised not only a lavish interior that spoke volumes about its owner, but also a multitude of makeovers brought about by changing fashions and occupants over the decades.

Even allowing for shifts in window proportions and pier widths, the house front changed little throughout the 18th century, especially when compared with what was to follow. And if the Regency façade saw more variation in the type of classical ornamentation applied, it nevertheless spoke the same language as its predecessors in the 18th century. The exciting scene-changes were generally confined to interiors within the existing building stock that Disraeli condemned for its own lack of adventure.

The 1840s, however, witnessed a plethora of styles applied to the town house and to both individual houses and to rows. The classical town-house aesthetic was itself taken to new extremes, as at Milner Square, London, where the continuous attic storey bands the houses together, while the loosely classical pilasters emphasize the verticality of the individual home. But at the same time, and nearby, new languages were being used, such as the Tudor styling that was applied to houses in Lonsdale Square. We tend, correctly, to associate this sort of period styling with suburbia, but here it was placed on a terrace of town houses. Elsewhere in London, Georgian architecture rubbed shoulders with Victorian insertions of remarkably different styles within one street. In Cheltenham, Wellington Square and Lypiatt Terrace

BELOW: Tudor styling at Lonsdale Square, in London, is an early hint of how the town house will be transformed. The gable returns, but it is offset, as the house front is divided into one wide and one narrow bay. It is not the styling that dictates the realignment at this point: the same was happening on many 'classical' town-house fronts.

ELDON SQUARE.

But we are not done with the classical yet. From the 1830s, the 'classical' was modelled less on the antique and more on the Italian Renaissance. Astylar buildings followed the model of Charles Barry's Reform Club (1837), with a rejection of superficial vertical emphasis in favour of a more integral horizontal design in the form of heavy cornices and other 'structural' devices. If Portland Place and Portman Square were respectable parents to the plain and weakling Baker, Harley and Wimpole Streets, as Disraeli suggested, they were outgrown in the 1840s by sturdier, more handsome offspring to the north-west in Belgravia and to the south-west in Brompton.

(both 1840s) shared the same basic classical form, with a higher and more elaborate centrepiece and flanking towers or pavilions beyond the longish wings; but the former had Gothic details, including crenellations, while the latter had the appearance of an unusually long Italian villa. The same contrast, achieved by the same means, could be found in Newcastle even earlier. The classicism of Eldon Square is what we have come to expect, but who could have foreseen the Tudor decoration of the more-or-less contemporary St Mary's Place?

There was little effect on planning – that came later in the century, when the town-house aesthetic was disrupted altogether. But the disruption began here, when the terraced house simply took off its classical dress and tried on something new. With hindsight, and as admirers of the classic English town house, we might see this 'development' as anything but – as an aberration, in fact. But in its own time, no doubt, it was exciting and progressive.

The speculative system under which huge new middle-class quarters were created may have changed little from the 18th century, but the houses themselves (although still classical) were noticeably different. They were generally bigger, and often better built at the upper end of the market. Their drawing rooms were more spacious and their bedrooms more numerous, to accommodate larger numbers of servants. Architecturally, they followed Nash in form and feature: they were classical, stuccoed and arranged in squares or crescents. Together, as Summerson says, they make the 'stucconia' in which the Veneerings of Charles Dickens' *Our Mutual Friend* had their super-affluent home.

There is certainly an obvious distinction between the London terraces of the 18th and 19th centuries, even if it is not always easy to articulate. Summerson puts it down to the influence of Barry's 'Italian Renaissance', which made them

more 'fulsome' than their predecessors. They certainly appear more solid (or stolid, if we are inclined to think negatively), less linear and, in a way, more affluent but less refined. They seem to have turned a little too far from the town-house ideal, making life in town too comfortable – it is no longer a crush.

There is some irony, however, as Summerson points out, that these houses with their 'air of inert affluence', the 'well-groomed residences of lawyers, doctors, engineers, manufacturers, city men of all kinds and of innumerable widows and spinsters', should now be 'busy honeycomb[s] of flats and bed-sitters'. In this respect they have often fared less well than their elder, plainer siblings.

These grand urban schemes were the last of the Georgian-style estate development in town. They remained urban – being within walking distance or an easy omnibus ride of the city, and, like their 18th-century predecessors, they drew

119

attention away from the inferior dwellings beyond and behind them. The manner in which adjacent estates were developed by ground landlords and speculative developers from the 17th century onwards remained an inescapable fact of London life. At the start of the 20th century, Hermannn Muthesius, sent by the German government to report on the state of English architecture, despaired at the mazes behind the capital's grander squares and streets:

Probably no area today provides a better idea of the medieval city than the network of streets in which the Englishman of the twentieth century lives. The cheerfulness with which he submits to the intelligence of the speculative builder in this matter is amazing.

But Muthesius admitted that the German capital had something to learn from the English regard for green urban spaces. If there is one major attitudinal difference between the classicizing 19th-century schemes and the brave, pioneering squares of the previous centuries, it is that they stand aloof from passing traffic by means of a broad strip of greenery between themselves and the avenue. They do not huddle together and hide their faces from the uncouth world. Even new squares were of such generous proportions that they barely registered as such. Many terraces in Leamington Spa, among them Lansdowne Crescent (1830s), included this green buffer, too, while a town's best terraces were sometimes set in their own parkland, as at Gambier Terrace, Liverpool, and Leazes Terrace, Newcastle.

BELOW: *Like many of its contemporaries, Lansdowne Crescent, Leamington, enjoyed a degree of detachment from the road as more terraced houses began to enjoy a parkland setting.*

THE AESTHETIC DISRUPTED

The Ousting of the Classic Town House

There was no one style or simple progression of styles in the second half of the 19th century. While it is easy to identify a change of taste in London's architecture from around 1870, it is difficult to articulate precisely what it involved. The names given to the various styles are loosely associative, and sometimes interchangeable, rather than being strictly descriptive or historically precise. What exactly was 'Queen Anne' in the first place, let alone in its revivalist manifestation? How typical of the Netherlands was 'Pont Street Dutch'?

BELOW: 'Dutch' styling is most evident at roof level in these Pont Street houses, revisiting the 'Holborn' gable of the 17th century.

121

ABOVE: *James Stuart's 1760s façade at 15 St James's Square, London, was an early example of architectural innovation there, as the need to refurbish or rebuild stimulated owners to mark the difference between themselves and their rather lacklustre neighbours.*

lar circumstances – that is, not where a whole new row was being erected, but where individual properties were ripe for reconstruction, as at St James's Square (see page 62) and Pall Mall. At the same time, it was demonstrated that those individual fronts responded very directly to the physical nature of the town house – tall and thin – and differentiated the house from its neighbours, while abiding by the same proportions and working within the same classical idiom. In this respect they were antithetical to the general aesthetic ambitions of the terrace.

The same thing happened in the second half of the 19th century, although the means of expression was entirely different. Even when neighbouring houses were built or rebuilt simultaneously and in similar styles, they did pull together for some greater good. Georgian ideals and Palladian rules and aesthetics were dismissed in favour of something more directly responsive to the individual house's verticality. Like the pre-classical house, these houses used a range of decorative devices to balance horizontality and verticality, with the latter tending to win, as gables once more dominated skylines.

The later 19th-century house responded to changes in fashion and to design movements both inside and out, to an extent that rarely happened in the Georgian period. Then, interiors changed fast, while exteriors – at least for much of the 18th century – changed slowly, if at all, and generally paid only lip service to fashion. The Victorian façade, on the other hand, often formed a full-blown response to new movements, and as the century wore on, house fronts were less 'façadist' and more an earnest reflection of a style or aesthetic that governed the whole building, such as 'Queen Anne' or 'Pont Street Dutch', the dominant styles of the 1870s. It is notable that older houses were not often given a new Victorian-style front, as they were in the Georgian age, although there are examples in the provinces. The new styles did not lend themselves so read-

In the end, descriptions of these styles tend to focus on individual elements and materials, many of which they shared: an abundance of red brick, loosely reminiscent of the 17th century; tall, white-painted sash windows loosely reminiscent of the earlier 18th century; and cut brick, stucco and terracotta used for decorative, textural effect, reminiscent of very little beyond other, contemporary houses.

By the 1870s, the period of urban (rather than suburban) expansion had ended, and building activity in town was now a matter of redeveloping, replacing and infilling. We saw how, in the later 18th century, the greatest innovation in town-house façades often occurred under simi-

ily to façadism. While the new Georgian front acted as an aesthetic screen, visually rationalizing all that lay behind it, the Victorian front was not so shallow, in any sense of the word. The logic of its arrangement was to accommodate, not to govern the disposition of the rooms behind. In its decoration, it protruded outwards and upwards, and adorned itself as and when it felt necessary and in a seemingly un-programmed way. It thereby put its own interests ahead of any allegiance to a row.

Adding Floors

Even the *internal* response of the 18th-century house to fashion was generally confined to applied decoration and fur-nishing, and the house-plan itself was little troubled. The town house at the upper end of the Georgian market, as we have seen, followed essentially the same format as that at the lower end, and all but the very largest of Victorian town houses did the same – they just had more floors. Except on limited building sites, grand, architect-designed houses no longer considered less to be more, or took the particularities of the typically long, narrow urban plot as their starting point. Instead they spread with self-satisfaction over deeper, wider sites, so that they had no need to have any-thing in common with either their prede-cessors or their contemporaries as far as planning was concerned. This may have

ABOVE: Although regularity of proportion still underlies these houses in Pont Street, London, the sleekness of the classic town-house aesthetic begins to lose out to the varied profiles of ornaments, elaborate gables and porches.

123

been just as well, as room types and numbers of servants increased, at least until the turn of the century, when servants were harder to come by. A move away from communicating rooms and towards increasingly separate and specialized spaces meant that those houses that stuck with the urban format of more length than width often used lightwells to allow greater building depth to be achieved on the site: lack of easy communication between front and back was no longer a problem, and conceivably an advantage.

The knock-on effect of adding more floors to the basic town house was that the neoclassical town-house façade was no longer optimally effective. Pilasters were in danger of looking not elegantly attenuated but unseemingly lanky as the house's relative tallness and thinness surpassed the capacity of standard formulae to cope with it. The perfect balance was lost. Horizontal emphasis therefore returned to

the architectural scene in the form of balconies, balustrades, decorative treatments for rows of windows and rustication. Variety in window shapes and surrounds distracted the eye, and a 'multitude of small accents' took the place of a few large ones. Mid-19th-century house designs from in and around Queen's Gate demonstrated the care required and the variety possible in articulating the façade of a three-bay, six- or seven-storey house. Loosely neoclassical details were used in various combinations to tie down rows of windows, as visual rather than classical logic requires. As a result, it was not always the first floor *piano nobile* that was distinguished by ornament: sometimes the second or even the third floor received the treatment. In this respect, these houses and others like them had less in common with their predecessors in London and more in common with much earlier Parisian town houses, where classical cor-

BELOW: *There is little regal about Royal Crescent, Scarborough, as the curve is insufficient to distinguish these houses from any other group of ordinary, individual houses of the period. Subsequent alterations and additions have not helped.*

rectness did not gain the upper hand over visual sense. These elevations looked neat enough in an outline drawing, but in reality the classical town house became overblown, overripe and past its best.

The problem of handling new extremes of verticality was solved from the 1870s by the abandonment of classicized fronts and the adoption of a variety of northern European forms that gave verticality full rein. Height could be emphasized, not disguised, with the help of prominent roofs, chimneys and a series of linear decorative devices, including pilasters with no classical reference point. Meanwhile, irregularity could be tolerated and accommodated in a plethora of small motifs, classical or otherwise.

Mid-range Town Houses

A major change to the town-house format occurred in the middle ranks. Practicality got the better of aesthetics when the ground floor of the smaller three-bay terrace house gave up its alignment with the floors above in favour of a door to one side with a single, wider window centred in the remaining width of the façade. With symmetry abandoned, and a door that no longer lined up with the windows above, there was more space for a decent-sized front room. The upper floors carried on as before, with narrower openings ranked in vertical strips. What might have been an awkward disjunction was ameliorated by distinguishing the ground floor with a different finish, usually stucco in imitation of rusticated stone. The pleasing result can still be seen in very many places, including at the gently curving terrace of modest stone-clad houses now out of their depth on Queen's Road, Reading.

This rational new approach went still further once classicism lost its grip on the façade of the terraced house. The elevation was vertically divided into a wide side, which was often occupied by a bay window rising through the storeys to cornice level, and a narrow one. This format appeared, often topped by a prominent

STUCCO

Stucco is a thin render used to give inferior masonry the appearance of finely dressed ashlar, at considerably less cost. Stucco finishes became popular for all or part of buildings in town and country from the early 1770s onwards. As 'palace fronts' became more prevalent in towns, stucco was drafted in to accentuate centrepieces and ends, which were often given additional decorative ornamentation, too, as at Mecklenburgh Square in London. Unfortunately, the quality of 18th-century stucco was often poor and prone to disintegration. This weakness has led to accusations of 'façadism' and analogies with make-up, which have done the 18th-century house no favours. But better renders were developed in the 19th century, and these were used in abundance in London, at the seaside and beyond.

BRICK AND TERRACOTTA

Local brick variations, advances in brick production and changing fashions all contributed to more variety in brick fronts over the centuries – and even within the 18th century itself – than might be guessed from row upon row of seemingly similar houses. But in the 19th century the decorative potential of brick was exploited to the full, as here at South Audley Street, London. At the same time, terracotta mouldings took over from Coade stone as a readily applied decorative medium, giving the overall (and sometimes oppressive) 'red' appearance of so many Victorian houses, in stark contrast to the prevailing whiteness of their stuccoed predecessors from the beginning of the century.

gable, in houses of all classes. An important consequence of this development was that it shot a large hole in the bows of the classic terrace treatment. Even though houses were still built to one basic design, the essential classical element of continuous horizontals at roof and storey levels was lost within it, and each house stood apart, however similar it might be to its neighbours. In time, a variety of 'vernacular' finishes, such as half-timbering, was given to gable fronts and other elements of the façade, offering further superficial distinctions between houses that were essentially the same.

Arts and Crafts

It is hard to say whether the new styles of the 1870s responded to or dictated the kinds of practical changes described above, but the two were well matched. The narrower bay to one side was not uncommon in the 17th-century façade, and its 19th-century revival therefore suited 'Queen Anne' or 'Pont Street Dutch' treatments, which did not give a hoot for symmetry. At the upper end of the market, many leading architects designed town houses with more or less condescension to urban conditions, and often for their artist friends. 'Artists' houses' were the urban cousins of the Arts and Crafts country houses. A Holland Park house by Philip Webb (1831–1915) for the artist Val Prinsep led the way, but the house that J. J. Stevenson (1831–1908) built for himself in Bayswater Road, which has since been bombed and demolished, received more publicity, and is generally considered the first 'Queen Anne' house in London. It was followed by Lowther Lodge, designed by Richard Norman Shaw (1831–1913). This house was perhaps stylistically important, displaying Shaw's style in town on a large canvas, but it was still more a country house than a town house. Shaw's houses in Kensington, Chelsea and Hampstead were more obviously urban. His house at 196 Queen's Gate (1875) set the trend for the 'Pont Street Dutch', which was much imitated by speculative developers in Kensington for the remainder of the century. The 'style' consisted of symmetrical groupings within an overall asymmetrical arrangement. The distinctive gable served not only to bind the arrangement together, but also to define the house as a single unit quite distinct from its neighbours. Despite some projections, this style of house retained the urban aesthetic of flatness and verticality, with the latter emphasized by superimposed, slim 'Dutch' pilasters. Shaw's trademark windows and the early northern Renaissance decoration give the whole a feel that was reminiscent of houses we last saw towards the end of the 17th century and at the same time distinctly Shavian and very much of the 19th century.

Pont Street Dutch therefore revived an English trend that predated the straitjacket of urban classicism, and looked at the same time to non-English sources for its inspiration. The result was something very much contrary to what we consider the archetypal English town house. Nevertheless, Hermann Muthesius argued that Shaw's houses:

> *... embody the spirit of the best type of rich Englishman: he has nothing of the parvenu about him and in his bearing he is the most modest and reticent of men. And at the same time these houses are the foundation-stones of a new architecture that disregards the now conventional idioms of past cultures fundamentally different from our own and no longer seeks identity in aristocratic embellishments but in unadorned simplicity.*

Note that Muthesius bands all northern Europeans together, so that the houses have a satisfyingly appropriate 'northernness' rather than a distressingly foreign 'southern-ness' – Italy is a long way from home. Like the moralizing theorists of the preceding century, Stevenson regretted that 'the foolish desire to be grander than we are' had led to a disregard for the 'natural' order of things in house façades. By the time Muthesius came to England, the

mood had turned against the classical 'trumpery' of pilasters and pediments, and towards the 'honesty' of vernacular building practice; by the 1880s in London and in about 1890 in Brighton, widely applied external stucco was almost wholly phased out. Muthesius focused on Shaw's larger houses at 180 and 185 Queen's Gate, and the comparison was really between these exceptional single houses and those aggrandized classical terraces, with all their palatial trappings (or 'aristocratic embellishments'). By comparison with a town house even at the upper end of the

BELOW: *Richard Norman Shaw revisits England's vernacular past at 196 Queen's Gate, London, with the design flair and skill appropriate to a professional architect of the 1870s.*

ABOVE: The hefty brick entrance to 52 Pont Street, London, and the vast white-painted wooden brackets looming above, may recall the 17th century in its materials, but not in the robustness of its style. And the intervening classic town house might never have happened.

plays the same game of general flatness disrupted by contrived projections – a reasonable compromise in town. Shaw's artistry combined red brick, white-painted sash windows and a variety of gables to produce four houses that were both sufficiently related and sufficiently different to give variety to a street while still acknowledging that they belonged to one. On the other hand, Stevenson, as Edward Jones and Christopher Woodward observe, 'was here trying the impossible: to design a terrace of houses while drawing attention to their individuality. As a result the façades are a mess of motifs'. That is, he evidently conceived them principally as a row, and secondly as individual houses. As a result, and unlike Shaw, Stevenson abided by the principle of consistent storey levels and relied on a more applied effect to add the differentiation he sought. In this respect he was, of course, closer to his Georgian predecessors.

All of these Cadogan Square buildings, and the very many like them elsewhere, have retained the essence of the town house – tall, relatively narrow, and preferably more-or-less flat to the street line – and sometimes highlighted it through gables and vertical motifs, while abandoning the governing classical aesthetic of the Georgian house. Much of our story of the town house is an account of that essence being alternately denied and emphasized through various means: we have seen both happen even within the period of the classic Georgian town house itself.

Meanwhile, in another blank space, Ernest George (1839–1922) created in Collingham and Harrington Gardens (begun 1881) houses so Dutch in appearance that Summerson describes them as 'a plausible reflection of the Amsterdam of Pieter de Hoogh'. The street houses of Amsterdam served well as a model, as they were not only tall and thin, but also varied in their outline and fenestration, as the desire for an individual family house was stressed by the individuality of the house itself. What is more, as Gavin Stamp and

Georgian market, Shaw's houses were huge. They relied on a wider range of elements – such as sheer size and variety of outline – to make an impact, whereas the Georgian house had the limited options of enhancing itself with applied decoration, banding together with its neighbours to look like more than the sum of its parts, or both.

The Dutch Influence

By the 1890s, central London was virtually full up. Cadogan Square was one of the few blank spaces left, and architects George Edmund Street (1824–1881), Shaw and Stevenson were all at work there. The asymmetry of Street's No 4 has more to do with Gothic Revival principles than with the calculated artistic-ness of the neighbouring Pont Street Dutch, but it

Colin Amery observed, 'their illiterate early Renaissance detail was highly attractive to Gothic renegades who feared the full panoply of the Classical Orders'. Even in early 19th-century Brussels, where a stricter classicism reigned, the houses of a row were often varied in height and cornice shape. Nevertheless, the houses at Harrington Gardens had unusually wide frontages to compensate for shallow depth, so they, too, were not strictly comparable with the standard Georgian town house. Ernest George's unnatural efforts here to make each house distinct from its neighbours, in the natural Dutch way, drew criticism from *Builder* magazine in 1883, which termed Harrington Gardens a 'sham antique collection of buildings'. The article continued:

> *Old streets do occasionally assume this kind of appearance of pieces of buildings in ever so many manners all muddled together, and they have a picturesque suggestiveness then, but to go about to make this kind of thing deliberately is child's play.*

There was clearly no winning way. Classicism was too foreign, too pretentious or too dull. Native and unaffected variety was preferable, but it had to come about naturally, which of course it hadn't since the 17th century and the rise of the speculative developer.

The Classical Resurgent

At the turn of the century, C. R. Ashbee (1863–1942) designed houses for Cheyne Walk, Chelsea, of which two survive – 38 and 39, which were built in 1899–1901. Although 38 is more interesting architecturally, it was designed specifically as a studio house and therefore had atypical needs in the context of this story. Number 39, however, was built speculatively, and demonstrates beautifully how windows can be used to emphasize horizontal or vertical lines, or to achieve a balance between the two. Here they are set so close as to almost form bands, especially at

second-floor level where six windows are squeezed in. The horizontal strips of windows are stacked up on each other, thus providing the necessary counter effect of verticality. Despite its unconventional variation in the number of windows on successive floors, the house front looks back to the late 17th or early 18th century

ABOVE: The unprecedented height of these buildings in Cadogan Square, London, effectively ruled out classical proportioning even if their architect, G. E. Street, had been that way inclined.

129

looked to the vernacular for design inspiration, the vernacular in town *was* the plainish Georgian town house, whether of the late 17th century or the 18th century. Ashbee was not alone in designing London houses in Georgian styles at the end of the century. The progression from 'Queen Anne' to neo-Georgian at this point was a logical re-enactment of the original development from the architecture of the late 17th and early 18th centuries to Palladianism.

Alastair Service highlights Sir Frank Elgood's contribution in this respect. He built 19 houses in Marylebone between 1891 and 1913, beginning with Queen Anne houses at 9 Harley Street and 81 Wimpole Street. The latter had the typically 'Queen Anne' features of superimposed, narrow, brick pilasters strapping the façade together; white-framed, narrow sash windows with a hint of roundness to their heads, which were pinned in place by keystones; and a gable. Two years later, Elgood's houses showed a distinct progression towards early classical forms, albeit in a wider façade, in a fanciful design that looks as if it was built over a century or more, but from the top downwards! It had three dormers with rather steep segmental pediments typical of 17th-century houses, or provincial town houses of the early 18th century. The second and third storeys had sash windows of early Georgian proportions. Then came an unusual extended Palladian window arrangement on the first floor, reminiscent of designs attributed to Sir Robert Taylor (1714–88) in the 1740s. Finally, at the bottom was a heavy polygonal bay window consuming two bays, in early 19th-century style, next to a sharply pedimented door case that reminds us where the house started: the late 17th century.

Instead of taking the Georgian house as a model, Elgood looked to it for inspiration. In his designs he revisited the glory days before imported Palladianism dampened all native creativity, and showed what could have been done if it had not

in its brickwork, plain casement windows, window heads and its general demeanour. The door hood adds greatly to this effect. It is both unusual and refreshing to see the early classical aesthetic getting a well-earned revival, and a relief from the sometime overstatement of Pont Street Dutch.

It is worth remembering that when such Arts and Crafts architects as Ashbee

been allowed to do so. At 11 Welbeck Street he even managed to create a Baroque terraced house – something that scarcely appeared in the Baroque period itself – and all in a two-bay façade. Again, there were elements of the house that owed something to his own time – and to earlier Pont Street Dutch – but Elgood's designs were firmly rooted in English architectural history. Elgood's own words on this subject offer a timely jolt to the classic English town-house enthusiast:

It is only natural that architects should … attempt to start afresh from the point when inventive genius gave place to mere copyism … The possibilities of the style seem infinite, and there is plenty of evidence that those who have the fortune to build in it are not trammelled with precedents and hard-and-fast lines. And yet the effect is generally quiet and pleasing, has a thoroughly English appearance and is entirely suited to modern requirements. But … this is not imitation of a past style. There is a wonderful originality in such designs and an entire absence of similarity or copying … who can say that it may not lead to what must be the desire of all, namely the formulating of a truly English 20th-century progressive architecture?

It falls to the next chapter to tell what actually happened in the 20th century, and what is happening in this one. But first we need to acknowledge that town-house construction was on the decline, as town life and architectural fashion found expression elsewhere.

ABOVE: *Sir Frank Elgood's façade at No 11 Welbeck Street, London, demonstrates his ability to use a variety of 'period' references to good effect in town-house fronts. Here the detailing is unusually Baroque, in keeping with the feel of the whole façade.*

OPPOSITE: *No 39 Cheyne Walk, London, combines Arts and Crafts elegance and simplicity with loosely historicizing references to create a front which would serve well as a model for future town houses.*

131

THE TOWN HOUSE ABANDONED

Town Flats and Suburban Villas

As early as 1867, purpose-built flats at Belgrave Mansions were erected on the Grosvenor Estate, and certainly by 1890 rebuilding in the capital focused on flats rather than houses, as did many new projects. The most famous of all these schemes is Shaw's Albert Hall Mansions (1879–86), built by a syndicate on ground belonging to the Commissioners for the 1851 Exhibition, although few major architects participated in this new trend. Mansion blocks were all the rage in the fashionable parts of the city and the inner suburbs, providing small bachelor (or spinster) apartments and flats for middle-class families not tempted by the suburbs but wanting to keep up a decent appearance in town.

The term 'mansion block' is telling. The sheer size of the blocks offered scope for artistic indulgence and splendour that the town house had scarcely been able to provide in all of its history. Albert Hall Mansions reworked the Dutch look to rather odd effect, while Edwardian Baroque and French Classical were favourite styles around 1900. Monumentally impressive exteriors together with opulent and spacious communal entrance halls created an air of stylishness and luxury that compensated for the size of the individual flats themselves. Whereas only relatively few people had ever been able to afford homes warranting the title, these were mansions for the many.

Hermann Muthesius reported on the foreign influences that had breached England's insularity in the last quarter of the 19th century:

> *... instead of the patriarchal family life of earlier times, many English families nowadays favour variety, freedom from encumbrances, liberty of movement, social distractions. It is for this section of modern*

England that flats exist. It is small, but because it floats on the surface it obtrudes itself upon even the most superficial observer of London life.

When country-house owners were tempted away from their rural comforts, the flat offered them 'greater flexibility of movement and the advantage that they need leave nobody in charge of the house when they return to the country or depart on their travels, nor have they the responsibility for the cost of keeping up a whole house, with roof and street-frontage.' Flats were the new 'lodgings', but purpose-built for the life led in and from them. Convenience took on a whole new dimension quite separate from that for so long associated with the town house. Blocks of flats disrupted the town-house ideal in every respect, and beat the palace-terrace at its own game. And, as Muthesius observed with some prejudice, 'by avoiding the artificiality of flat-life a man merely condemns himself to what is perhaps the greater artificiality of running one of the cramped, six-storeyed London terrace-houses'.

The town house faced challenges from other quarters, too. The predominant theme of domestic architecture in the period from between Waterloo and the start of the Second World War was increasingly suburbia, not the town. The suburb had developed earlier in England than elsewhere, once town walls had lost their importance. Much of the 18th-century West End was effectively a suburb, in its division of residence from business. But the suburb only began to take on a separate identity somewhere between town and country in the 19th century, as transport expanded the distance that could be considered near enough *to* yet far enough *from* work. By late century, the upper and middle classes in the new industrial and commercial towns lived in the suburbs rather than in a terrace at the centre of town. And although it crops up in some odd places, the classic English town house is not often found in the suburbs proper,

where there was a different role and a very different aesthetic at play. To begin with, in the outer reaches of the urban areas, buildings maintained their stylistic and formal links with the town house, as we have seen. But the further out development spread, the more scope and demand there was for a new architecture of suburbia. Clifton, in Bristol, may have had its share of grand terraces, and for good topographical reasons, but adjacent Redlands specialized in suburban villas – tall, bulky, and consuming more ground space. Just as most of the interesting pattern-book designs are for villas, so in practice most architectural experiment took place in new suburban building types. For this reason, the suburbs are another book altogether.

ABOVE: *At Lansdown Court, Cheltenham, semi-detached Italian villas of the 1830s make a break from the terrace formula, even though elements of group composition (here, the towers at either end) remain in force.*

CONCLUSION
A Return to Freedom

The late 19th and early 20th centuries witnessed something of what was going on before the classic Georgian house hit us hard. Especially when the classic format was annihilated, there was a return to a freedom of expression on house fronts akin to that of the 16th and 17th centuries, even if it was less a personal expression related to the occupant and more a formula applied to a row or a stylized scheme for an individual house.

In this respect, the 'classic' period can seem a deviation, something that gets in the way of a natural, English development. Ernest George certainly thought so. The classic English town house may be distinctly English, in the way that urban domestic classical architecture was manifested, but it can easily stand accused of being distinctly un-English in its constituent elements and in their treatment.

It is worth noting, however, that in recent decades we have not harked back to the Victorian and Edwardian eras, but to the Georgian era instead. As we will see in the next chapter, where new housing looks to the 19th century, it is to the suburban villa, which was, for a while, the standard approach to the four- or five-bedroom family house on new residential estates. For the town house, though, the Georgian house remains the model. Whether in imitation of the city terrace or the provincial merchant's house, the new urban house is inextricably and favourably linked with the Georgian period.

LEFT: *On the basis of this composition at Pont Street, London, it is hard to say that freedom from 18th-century architectural principles is always a good thing.*

OPPOSITE: *Early 19th-century architecture perpetuating the trends of the preceding century at Windsor Terrace, Bristol.*

CHAPTER FIVE

A CLASSIC STYLE FOR A MODERN AGE

The Town House After 1914

In the earlier part of the 20th century the strive for modernity left the classic English town house out in the cold. Architectural responses to the need for housing density took the form of purpose-built flats and so England initially looked to the Continent rather than its own culture for architectural inspiration. Where space was not an issue – for example, in the suburbs – the house looked to its own domestic architectural history and played with a range of loosely vernacular and historicizing styles to which even the most determined town-house architecture could never give full expression. But the town house was not done with, and the later half of the 20th century and the first few years of the 21st century have seen the 'classic' house conceived as a classic for the first time. Existing houses have been given new leases of life, while the popularity of the town-house aesthetic has proved the saving of property developers involved in new-builds.

Coutts Crescent, London

BREAKING FREE
The Town House Without Historicism

Many terraced houses are today given the name 'town house' by estate agents and developers; however, only some of these fall into the town-house category as described in this book. But why does this paradigm persist even in essentially non-urban residential developments? Is there a recognized consumer demand for this type of building, or has the push come principally from the developers? The town house has three principal and related characteristics: flexibility of space, stacked accommodation and housing density. The latter quality is certainly an attraction to developers keen to maximize profit without resorting to the very different market for apartments.

BELOW: The villa model for a row of town houses persists in the 20th century at Willow Road, Hampstead, London. The strong horizontal emphasis belies the internal division into three vertical homes.

The first half of the 20th century witnessed the lowest ebb of the town house – it was neither a popular type of new-build, nor a promising focus for renovation and refurbishment. In many locations across the country, streets that had once been smart, such as Plymouth's Union Street, became seedy, and the classic town house

was devalued. Nevertheless, this type of house did not die out altogether, but was expressed differently, if not in a widespread manner. There was no doing without the town house, even if apartment blocks and the burgeoning suburbs decreased demand for this type of structure in some quarters.

London in the Modern Era

Much of the most interesting work was completed in London, particularly the north of the capital. A terrace of three houses at Willow Road, Hampstead (1938), was a Modernist take on the classic English terrace house by Erno Goldfinger (1902–97). Like many of its 18th-century counterparts, the development was reminiscent of a contemporary villa, with a distinct horizontal emphasis at first-floor level that had much in common with Continental horizontal living. Nevertheless, the occupants lived 'vertically' between the party walls, in the English manner. The first floor formed a *piano nobile*, which was raised above garage accommodation, a formula followed by many later 'town houses', whether located

in town or not. An even earlier group of houses, built at Genesta Road, Plumstead in 1933–34 by Berthold Lubetkin (1901–90) and A. V. Pilichowski, adopted the format of the classic town house in a similar way, layering the accommodation, with the garage shunting the principal rooms to first-floor level. At around the same time, Francis Lorne erected a terrace of houses at 4–10 Wells Rise, St John's Wood, which gave a Modernist twist to the almost suburban town-house-cum-villa so typical of the area's later 18th- and 19th-century development.

Housing built some while later in 1979 by Jeremy Dixon (born 1939) at 103–123 St Mark's Road, London, demonstrates a remarkable grasp of the town house's essence and the architecture of the streetscape, while expressing neither in a classical idiom. With markedly pitched gables and bays, these houses have more in common with their Queen Anne predecessors in the 19th century (see pages 121-123), although their demeanour proves quite different. Meanwhile, steep steps to raised entrances make reference to the stuccoed houses of the 1830s and 1840s,

ABOVE: *A one-off design to satisfy particular client needs at Red House, Tite Street, London, frees the architect from the restrictions governing the London house interior. The street front makes reference to the history of town-house fronts in London, with its double-height* piano nobile.

have seen so often before, create the illusion of a single, substantial and impressive unit.

More recently, a terrace of 11 houses by Proctor Matthews Architects at Ropemaker Field, London (1996), took a different approach, akin to classicism but again expressed in a distinctly modern way. The façades are layered and the windows closely grouped, giving each house a vertical emphasis. The undisguised attic storey is not concealed behind a parapet, yet it has something of both the parapet and the cornice about it in the way it levels the building. Balconies emphasize the first-floor *piano nobile*. The format and aesthetic of the later 18th-century house was the point of reference for this development, even if there is no hint of historicism about the result.

As ever, rebuilding offers most licence for distinction in the individual house, and many modern and post-modern responses to 18th-century town-house architecture keep company with the very buildings they address in their façades. In 2002, Tony Fretton Architects erected Red House in Tite Street, London, which was unlike anything seen before, but nevertheless referential in its materials and composition to 18th- and 19th-century predecessors in the area. Its most striking feature is a double-height *piano nobile*, which, like Lady Isabella Finch's house at 44 Berkeley Square (see page 52), left little space for other rooms; but, like its illustrious predecessor, it was not designed for family life.

while having nothing of their pomp and stolidity. Material variety is the key to the articulation of the façade. Despite 18th-century complaints that town-house fronts were inherently deceptive and therefore dishonest, the deliberate emphasis on the house fronts at St Mark's Road is actually the most honest approach of all.

Closest of all to retaining the town-house aesthetic is a splendid terrace of 11 four-storey town houses in the shallow Coutts Crescent, London, a development designed by Chassay Wright Architects in 1986–89. The emphasis of these large individual houses lies in the strong verticals rising from ground level, along with piers and grouped windows. But the verticality of the houses is tempered by a continuous attic storey running along the top of the development with little interruption. The end houses were designed with additional studio bedrooms, and the 'towers' thus formed fix the row in place and, as we

A PERENNIAL ANSWER

The Town House Reborn

Beyond London, on suburban housing estates of the 1960s and 1970s, the term 'town house' began to take on a new meaning, which still adheres in some contexts today. It remained a byword for spatial economy and vertical living, but the 'classical' connotations were dropped. Like the modernist houses discussed above – although lower down the social order – the estate town house was modern through and through, often incorporating a garage at ground-floor level, with reception rooms thereby raised to the first-floor level.

But this was no emulation of a *piano nobile* and its associations of grandeur, or at least classiness, just a response to a different and very modern need. Estate agents still refer to these structures as 'town houses', partly out of habit no doubt, but also, I suspect, because the term lends some distinction to what is otherwise fairly ordinary and hardly classy building stock.

Since the 1980s, developers have often included some sort of terraced housing as part of a mixed portfolio of building stock on new estates. At first these were two-storey starter homes (still designated

LEFT: *Banners on a convex crescent of 'Regency' terraced houses at Sherfield Park, near Basingstoke, tempt passers-by with a 'classic' look and offers of part-exchange and cash back.*

ABOVE: *Burton Crescent, now Cartwright Gardens, near King's Cross, London, displays a much-executed terrace format: a raised, rusticated and stuccoed ground floor, with round-headed openings, two plainer but decent storeys above, and an attic. The mix of two- and three-bay houses is masked by the continuous rows at first- and second-floor levels. Engraving by Robert Dennis Chantrell, 1813.*

'town houses'); now they are often three or even four-storey family homes. And, most importantly, they have readopted a classical dress. The terraced house, more particularly the 'town house', is no longer viewed solely as a starting point to be moved away from as soon as possible. It has regained some of its credibility in the housing market, both as a new-build and through refurbishment.

Why has this happened? Looking at the current new-build market, we find something very similar to what we saw in the 18th century – the tall, slim house suits both developers and buyers alike, and it is difficult to say which leads the other.

Government planning policy introduced in 2000 set minimum density targets for developers, legislating for the most efficient use of land. A row of three- or four-storey houses is the most effective use a developer can make of space in a house-based residential development. Detached houses with separate garages and substan-

tial gardens to the front and rear are now inevitably outnumbered on new developments by such houses. Many developers have met the challenge head on, and now boast of their 'town houses' above all building types: in a news release of February 2005, Stamford Homes reported 'a growing portfolio of townhouses … which not only fit with the planning policy, but whose eye-catching designs, architectural features and innovative styles are pleasing customers.' The Peterborough-based developer claims to have 'answered public demand, as well as responding to government planning guidelines, with three-storey homes now being built on almost all its developments'. One new development is 'dominated by town-houses'. Town-house properties are, Stamford Homes states, increasingly popular – and there is no reason to doubt that this is the case. As with the 18th-century town house, innovation is born of limitation, in this case the legislative framework. Within

it, Stamford indicate that they have 'been able to design some genuinely exciting properties which include rooms in the roof, garden rooms … first floor lounges, offices for homeworking and roof top terraces'.

The designs are generally 'urbanized', because one cannot build either a three-bed semi or use a style reminiscent of it at that density. The classic town house formula therefore comes into its own. Window and door proportions are old knowledge that has been reused and is guaranteed to work. The trend away from applied finishes and trims, and towards design inherent in the built form, leads once more to a Georgian restraint. It is certainly hard to imagine how such buildings could have been marketed without borrowing something of the cachet of the classic English town house. What a gift to developers! Small wonder that terminology designed to invoke still more associations than the house front itself is promi-

nent in the promotional literature. How else could a developer hope to sell even high-standard terraced houses as luxury homes?

The Royal Crescent Revisited

Under the topical heading 'Grand Design', Bewley Homes' 2005 newspaper advertisement for 15 four-bedroom 'Georgian-styled' town houses at The Crescent, Cadugan Place, Reading, aims high with its references (if ultimately somewhat wide of the mark it sets itself with its architecture): 'Reminiscent of The Royal Crescent in Bath, this distinguished collection of four-storey, four-bedroom town-houses has been inspired by the past, yet designed for today's lifestyle'. Frankly, the reminiscence is limited to The Crescent's expected curve and a very general classical styling externally. It has much closer counterparts at, for example, Cartwright Gardens (formerly Burton Crescent), near London's King's Cross. But such a brave

ABOVE: The Crescent at Cadugan Place, Reading, looks more to 19th-century prototypes such as Burton Crescent than to its 18th-century predecessors in Bath and elsewhere. Despite being 'luxury' homes, the houses are only two bays wide, and of four rather than five storeys. Nonetheless, the high specification of their finishes together with their price tags marks them out as superior properties.

143

comparison strikes the right note of exclusivity, classic styling and, ironically, given what we know of buildings in Bath, quality. No-one but the architectural historian investigating the classic English town house would give the comparison any serious analytical attention. With steep steps leading to a raised ground floor, The Crescent in Reading is far more reminiscent of 19th-century Belgravian terraces than of 18th-century Bath in this respect. But that connection has less immediate punch than a link with the greatest of Georgian cities.

The Cadugan Place Crescent is also said to be 'inspired by the classical Georgian … residences which surround the area', and purports to bring the purchaser 'signature, modern living space within striking period-styled architecture all within walking distance of Reading's vibrant and cosmopolitan town centre'. Deriving inspiration from and complementing local period architecture is important – not for ethical reasons, but simply because buyers are more likely to buy period-style town houses if they are accustomed to the whole town-house aesthetic and vertical living, if only from an external point of view. Market experts say that new town houses sell best in areas where there is existing older town-house stock – that is, where people are familiar with the aesthetic and perhaps the vertical living element of town houses, and there is thus something to emulate. Where town houses are no longer or have never been part of the urban picture, there is little demand for their modern counterparts, and blocks of flats are more likely to answer the need for housing density.

Unlike its 18th- and 19th-century predecessors, the modern classic town house has no basement. All-important 'service' accommodation is incorporated in the main body of the house – it is cheaper to build from the ground floor up than to dig down. More importantly, there is less need to keep domestic goings-on away from the householder's delicate senses, as those services are now cleaner and less space consuming. Washing and drying machines can be tucked away in a utility room – but not too far away, as there are no longer servants to manage them. At Cadugan Place the 'service' accommodation is partly at ground level, along with the garage, in a modern-day approximation to the classic town-house format. The developers call this the 'lower ground floor', which

BELOW: Floor plans for terraced houses at Cadugan Place, Reading.

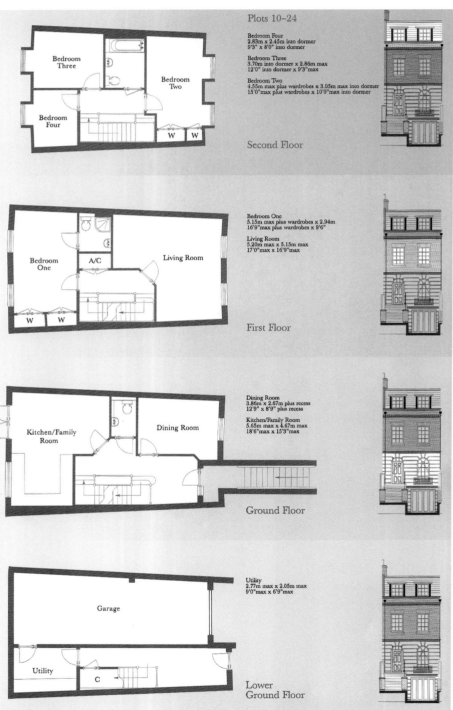

Plots 10–24

Bedroom Four
2.83m x 2.45m into dormer
9'3" x 8'0" into dormer

Bedroom Three
3.70m into dormer x 2.86m max
12'0" into dormer x 9'3" max

Bedroom Two
4.55m max plus wardrobes x 3.05m max into dormer
15'0" max plus wardrobes x 10'0" max into dormer

Second Floor

Bedroom One
5.15m max plus wardrobes x 2.94m
16'9" max plus wardrobes x 9'6"

Living Room
5.20m max x 5.15m max
17'0" max x 16'9" max

First Floor

Dining Room
3.86m x 2.67m plus recess
12'9" x 8'9" plus recess

Kitchen/Family Room
5.65m max x 4.67m max
18'6" max x 15'3" max

Ground Floor

Utility
2.77m max x 2.05m max
9'0" max x 6'9" max

Lower Ground Floor

not only hints at the half-basement of the period home, but also conveniently leaves the dining room and kitchen on the 'ground floor', and thus the living room on the 'first floor'. In this way, even nomenclature is drafted in to reinforce links with the classic house. But this name allocation is contradicted by the exterior finish of the structures. Although the 'ground' and 'first floor' here are equal in height, the channelled 'stone' finish, together with an elevated position, emphasizes the importance of the lower of these two floors. Looking at the building, we would expect the living room to be on this 'stone' level – perhaps at the back, to make the best use of space, with the dining room at the front, as it is. We would expect only bedrooms and bathrooms on the top two storeys. But this is really nitpicking, and the Crescent at Cadugan Place is a commendable modern take on the classic English town house. The houses strike a successful balance between the 'town house' of the 1960s and 1970s and the classic town house of the 18th and early-19th centuries, with their integral garage, raised living accommodation, classical references and emulation of hierarchical living.

At the Croudace development at Sherfield Park, outside Basingstoke, three- and four-storey houses abound, and the names of each of the house styles reinforce historical associations. The substantial 'Merchant House' is a four-storey Georgian-style house of the type found in provincial towns. The 'Townhouse' is similar, but built over three storeys. But it is the terraced 'Regency' which is grouped in a shallow convex crescent at the site's entrance to entice buyers in. All estates require a bold frontage development, and the joint impact of a row of taller houses does the job well. Period styling and labelling speak of quality and excellence – if you don't know the real story behind the 18th-century town house, the associations are all good ones.

Although 'Regency' town houses are used to sweep passing traffic onto the estate, there is no question of buyers being forced into a corner by the renaissance of the multi-storey home. While not everyone is prepared to become accustomed to first-floor reception rooms, or living over more than two floors, the up-and-down spatial experience is surely part of the house's appeal for many purchasers. Developers seem to agree that the more affluent young professionals are the main

ABOVE LEFT AND RIGHT: The Merchant House (left) and the Townhouse (right) at Sherfield Park, near Basingstoke, look to provincial prototypes. If they form part of a terrace, it is likely to comprise a diverse collection of loosely Georgian house styles and types, somewhat in keeping with their chosen model.

ABOVE: A terrace of generously proportioned two-bay terraces at Poundbury, near Dorchester, seems to float above the ground. The temporary-looking steps against the black base rather detract from the clean effect of the main body.

market for town houses, but they also appeal to 'mature sole occupants or couples looking for an alternative to the traditional "box" home with garage and garden'.

Versatile and Flexible

Versatility and flexibility are words that feature time and time again in developers' and agents' blurb for three- or four-storey houses, and for good reason. But it is unclear whether flexibility in this form is what people want, or whether the developers are persuading people that is what they want, because that is what they now need to give them. Much play is made of the town house's scope for tailoring itself to its occupants' specific needs at any one stage of occupancy. The house's compartmentalization is again at the core of its flexibility, and room designations are suggested rather than fixed. This flexibility is also part of a move to 'design for life': the owner of a new town house need never move – the new town house can offer him everything he needs at any stage of his life.

The ability of the town house to be self-contained also suits the commuter-based society of the late 20th and 21st centuries. As we have seen before, a small footprint leads to optimum convenience and compactness. What is more, grounds are small, and therefore easy to maintain, while the owners can benefit from the landscaping that inevitably and wisely comes with these new out-of-town town houses, as developers are not slow to point out.

Although the 18th-century consumer may well have been attracted by the density of accommodation in a good London street or square – one can never be too close to prestigious neighbours – it might seem unlikely that the same quality has the equivalent appeal on a modern housing development. But research has shown not only that intrusive noise is not necessarily a function of higher density, but also that people do not perceive privacy as we think they might: they are more concerned about getting away from each other within their individual dwellings than with the proximity or even noise of neighbours. The new-style town house offers the type of internal zoning that appeals to purchasers, while its close grouping with its fellows is not considered a particular dis-

advantage. In a commendably upbeat way, Stamford Homes report that 'higher density also lends itself to the creation of more communities, giving people the chance to meet and get to know their neighbours'. Inside the house, 'young couples are creating more private rooms for guests or for working from home, families are spreading themselves out – giving over the top floor of the house to teenagers and their loud music'. Certainly, if well managed, vertical living can mitigate the feeling of being cramped.

Parking and Planning

Of course the new town house obviates for the modern consumer those irritating inconveniences of the older house – parking is either incorporated in the house itself, as at The Crescent, Cadugan Place, or assured in nearby garages and secure lots, as at Sherfield Park and Poundbury, in Dorset. Legislation restricts spaces to 1.5 per house, regardless of house size. Croudace and other developers improve the street scene by grouping spaces in rear courtyards, or by building garages behind houses with bedrooms or work accommo-

dation over them. To call these 'mews' would be a waste of a good marketing term – people belong in mews now, and no matter whether the buildings they comprise bear any relation to those designed for the original occupants of mews: horses, stable boys and carriages. The cachet of the mews, as a marketing term, is even harder to pin down than the cachet of the term 'town house', because it fails to conjure up a generic and ideal image against which the product to be purchased can be compared. What's more, new-built mews buildings now front main roads, so that – as with the town house in some instances – even siting is not a factor in the link between past and present, marketing term and conjured-up image. As far as the town house is concerned, the prominence of references to garages and secure parking is not as cringingly anachronistic as it first seems: adverts for the smartest of London homes in the 18th century often mentioned accommodation for horses and carriages before that for people.

The crescents at Poundbury or at Sherfield Park, like many unified or palace-fronts before them, are less a visual

ABOVE: *A trio of two-bay town houses at Poundbury relies on stock devices to turn it into an architectural unit: widely spaced pilasters form a composition in the upper storeys, while the ground floor is distinguished by a different finish. Somewhat unfortunately, the dark central drainpipe divides the lower part into two uncomfortably asymmetrical halves.*

ABOVE: *An early example of the town house 'out of town' at Park Town Circus, Oxford. Here, the desire for a circus seems to have come ahead of the need for closely bunched houses, whereas today the reverse is generally true.*

trick than a statement of self-satisfaction in the security of a group identity. What these new developments are unlikely to see (possibly on pain of expulsion at Poundbury, where the buildings are effectively 'listed') is any effort on the part of current or subsequent owners to differentiate the external presentation of these houses from their immediate neighbours. Admittedly, town houses at Poundbury could be differentiated by the simple omission of the apparently statutory potted and clipped bay tree outside the front door. But these house fronts will never see the type of architectural experiment witnessed in St James's Square and on Pall Mall in the 1760s and 1770s, which were a direct response to the peculiarities of the town-house front. Perhaps, also, the uniform front is now taken as the essence of the town house, in the absence of other factors, especially

where interior references to the classic town house are largely reduced to two sash windows in reception rooms.

The result of the planning regulations is that the urban look – the original response to the practical need for high-density building – is everywhere, even in the most rural of locations. One is hardly in the urban thick of things at Poundbury, and even less so at Sherborne St John. Terraces have long appeared outside town as an economical way of building a group of houses, but such terraces didn't necessarily follow urban fashions, often being more vernacular in reality or imitation. In essence, the town house evolved from the vernacular terraced house, adopted some classical principles and became more standardized because legislation focused on towns, speculators were more likely to build in larger numbers there, and because

housing abutted adjacent housing and therefore followed its lead. What's different in these new developments is how the town house aesthetic is transported way beyond even the suburbs and out into the country. It is clear that today's 'town house' tag (at least among developers) comes down to the aesthetic itself, which comprises two things: the façade and the vertical living.

The town houses on new estates imitate not only smarter terrace developments in major towns and cities, but also the more independent Georgian town house, as found in smaller towns, where there was no large-scale, organized development. On the Poundbury Estate, for example, this type of mix of the more vernacular with the stylized classical house is emulated, albeit rather unsatisfactorily. The same is found at Sherfield Park, creating an effect not

unlike groups of individual merchant houses at North Brink, Wisbech, for example. The classical town house in this context is rather grander than its neighbours: distinct and aloof. The true town-house aesthetic, which I have argued is to be found fully expressed in the grander Georgian terrace house, is not what is sought after here. Rather, it is the 'classic' element that appeals – and that very aloofness.

It is notable that the Victorian town-house façade or style is rarely adopted for town-house architecture in the present day. As we have seen, it actually has much more to do with Englishness than the restrained Georgian terrace-house façade ever did. But at Cadugan Park, the family homes are 'Georgian' terraced houses, while the flats are purpose-built and purpose-divided 'Victorian' urban/suburban villas. Of course, both types of older

ABOVE: Merchant houses at Wisbech find themselves precursors of the amalgam of Georgian house types in today's picturesque 'urban villages'.

ABOVE: The huge, gently convex Lansdown Crescent, Cheltenham, of the 1830s, manages to be remarkably unified despite its great length. Many such terraces have fallen on good times in the last 30 years, with a demand for flats in period properties. Developers have rescued some from near dereliction.

these economic factors, as a result, really, of the very same economic factors that brought it into being in its classic form. Rejuvenation of some inner city areas is heavily based on the classic English town house's appeal – it scrubs up well. The Georgian town house and its hierarchical living space make it eminently suitable for conversion to flats, so that all the positive points about flats to which Hermann Muthesius drew our attention are accommodated in the converted classic English town house. A publication of 1947 – *Houses into Flats: Key to Conversion* – concludes that 'the converted Georgian or Victorian house thoughtfully planned around the daily needs of the proposed tenants, offers a home more in keeping with the needs of a boisterous family than does the boxy accommodation of the average modern block'.

The classic English town house was always an adaptable product, and the trend to convert rows of town houses for apartment living is just the latest manifestation of an ever-present exploitation of the town house's spatial flexibility. As we have seen, one family per house was an ideal not always attained in the 18th century, and the ranking of storeys was equivalent to the ranking of inhabitants. Nowadays a first-floor flat will always be marketed for more than a ground-floor flat; a ground-floor flat for more than a lower-ground, basement or attic flat, even if the only real difference is in ceiling height and not square footage. Occupation of part of a Georgian town house is our nearest parallel to the supposed charms and appeal of the palace front: we can delude ourselves that we occupy a whole house, in turn part of a much larger building, when we really only have a handful of rooms, sometimes below ground. And the refurbished, converted Georgian house with 'original features' – including draughty, rattling sash

building are converted to flats, but it is interesting that this divide prevails.

The Classic Town House Today

So much for new houses; what is happening to the existing classic English town house? Low-density housing types, such as 1930s bungalows and post-war semis, are more likely to come under threat than high-density town houses, as the value of the plot of land on which a dwelling stands begins to exceed house value in these areas. The town house seems safe from

windows – is differentiated in the market from the modern purpose-built apartment blocks in just the same way as the 18th-century house with its modern sashes differentiated itself from neighbouring older building stock.

At the top end of the market, the classic town house may not appeal to the rich international purchaser, less enamoured of vertical living than the wealthy Englishman and more prominent at this end of the market. According to Charlie Smith of Sotheby's International Realty, 'When they are spending millions, they don't want a third of the property taken up with a staircase and landings'. He talks, too, of his difficulty selling a luxury town house in Belgravia: it has a roof terrace and parking, 'but it is on seven floors and it is at best 17 feet (5 metres) wide, and buyers say it is not for them'. In stark economic terms, 'prime London flats are now more expensive than houses, in terms of price per square foot'. As in the 18th-century, convenience is sometimes related inversely to size.

A TASTE FOR LATERAL LIVING

An article in the 'Property' section of the *Daily Telegraph* in June 2005 raised the question: 'Has the London town house lost its cachet?' We are talking here about a very small percentage of both the national building stock and the housing market, but the feature suggests that the 'demand for a posh place in town has fallen'. The principal focus of the report – No 31 Belgrave Square – is hardly a typical town house, though, even by London standards. Marketed at £33 million, the four-bay property offers 21,000 square feet (1,951 square metres) of space in a prestigious location, and has '10 bedrooms, 11 bathrooms, a kitchen designed for a team of chefs, an eight-person lift and state-of-the-art technology … a pool in a garden room, a four-bedroom mews and a media studio across the top floor'. It offers purchasers a sense of space at odds with the more typical vertical experience. The article suggests that 'the London market has developed a taste for lateral living', although most buyers look for it in a more modestly priced flat rather than a multi-million-pound house.

CONCLUSION
An All-round Performer

So, the classic English town house has some failings after all, but its guest appearance in many new residential developments – many of them not remotely urban, even if sometimes styled 'urban villages' – is apparently a success story.

It is hard to pin down exactly what drives developers to include rows of town houses in eclectic mixes of housing types, styles and sizes. The developers themselves often seem unsure, but C G Fry & Son, builders of a large proportion of the ultimate 'urban village', Prince Charles' pet project Poundbury, in Dorset, claim in their promotional literature that a four-bedroom town house in the 'much acclaimed "crescent"' has 'always proved popular' in the development, and moreover 'gives pur-chasers the opportunity to belong to a very exclusive group of house buyers'. It is odd how exclusivity is now, and always has been, in the town-house market, achieved through huddling the dwellings together rather than spacing them apart. It remains not just the house itself, but also its group identity that lends it a certain cachet. And it is hard to think of any other domestic building type that really gains rather than loses from a group identity and very close neighbours.

BELOW: *The Crescent, Poundbury, groups houses of varying plans yet consistent styling to good scenic effect.*

AN ENDURING ATTRACTION

Where next for the town house? Are the out-of-town town houses rising on the new developments just the latest, or in fact the *last* incarnation of the classic town house? The links between such new houses and the classic Georgian house are often tenuous in any case.

BELOW: *A house at Crown Street, Stamford, is 18th century underneath and early 19th century on top, combining Gothick glazing-bars, canted bays and a Tuscan porch.*

In the new-build world, the label 'town house' is intended to conjure up an appearance and layout, which, while deriving from *real* town-house architecture, now operates entirely independently of a town location. The terms, 'Georgian', 'Regency' and even 'town house' are essentially a form of shorthand, which sends a positive message to buyers untroubled by its vagaries. Will the latest legislative straitjacket inspire architects to come up with new solutions to questions of population density? The modern ideal might be a house embodying all the convenience and versatility of the classic house, but replacing the historical styling with something equally appealing. We have already seen experiments to this end, notably in the earlier part of the 20th century, when architects learned to split the classical atom into proportion and style, retaining only the former in their town-house designs. But the new aesthetic did not catch on. Like everything subsequent to the 18th-century house, it was not looked back to, or taken as a model for future development. Designers have yet to come up with an exterior design good enough – or broadly appealing enough – to rival the classic town house façade, in the open market at least. We don't call the Georgian town house a classic for no reason. It remains a constant point of reference – a benchmark against which all other 'town'-houses must be measured, and against which most fail.

What makes the Georgian town house

153

ABOVE: *Brunswick Square, Brighton, is distinctly reminiscent of John Nash's work at Regent's Park, London.*

'classic'? Why do these houses please us? We have already considered some reasons why they pleased the Georgians themselves, but it seems that there is not so much overlap between their reasons and ours as might be expected. Certainly we share a common satisfaction with the proportions of the town-house façade, but while we positively admire it, the 18th-century house buyer simply accepted the design as a default situation. The relationship between class and taste may have helped in the general appeal of classicism in the Georgian era, which accounts for so many classicized fronts stuck on earlier buildings. In our own time, even more than its own, 18th-century classicism is accepted, without much thought, as 'good taste'.

On the other hand, we also have some delight in the mismatch between front and back, which so troubled many Georgian architectural critics. It is hard to say whether 'vertical living' appealed to the Georgian town-dweller as it does to so many of us, but what we do see then and now is general satisfaction with the architectural answer to the fundamental and now perennial problem of the shortage and cost of land.

In his report on the English house at the end of the 19th century, Hermann Muthesius echoed 18th-century critics in his disappointment with the English town house:

It is in the nature of things that the town house, which is dependent upon drastic measures and arbitrary conditions, cannot be a natural end-product of the development of the house. Its merit is limited and it is far inferior in importance to the freely evolved country house.

But unlike the 18th-century critics and Muthesius, we are free from the country-house paradigm, as it is no longer part of our conceptual framework. We appreciate the aesthetic of the town house in its own right – we are used to it and we want it. We have the benefit of understanding that the town house in its classic form is an abnegation of everything to do with the country. It is emphatically urban and gives itself over to the constraints of its urban environment. That is a good part of its attraction, even where it appears in less-than-urban settings.

There is no getting away from the fact that people love Georgian houses. Most of us cannot hope to own a country house, but a period town house seems relatively modest – despite its high price tag in better areas – and therefore accessible. It doesn't seem too much to ask for. In Vita Sackville-West's *All Passion Spent* (1931), the 88-year-old Lady Slane, as her first demonstration of very belated independence, moves to a small, red-brick Georgian row house in Hampstead, which first took her notice 30 years before. Of course, it is there unchanged. 'It was a convenient little house', Lady Slane remembers, 'not too small and not too large'. Her maid 'could manage it single-handed … with perhaps a daily char to do the rough work'. The house is actually not that small: 'Bedrooms, three; bathroom, one; lavatories, two; reception rooms, three; lounge hall [sic]; usual offices. … Half an acre of garden … Fine cellar'. But it is still described as 'modest'. Externally at least, the house also sends visitors a definite message. On her friend Mr FitzGeorge's first visit, he 'had paused in front of Lady Slane's house, and with the eye of a connoisseur had appreciated its Georgian dignity. "Ah," he said with satisfaction, "the house of a woman of taste."' (He changes his mind when he goes inside.) The façade of the Georgian house is safe from criticism; its aesthetic merits are a given.

The classic English town house responded to the conditions of its making. But along the way its design, form and appearance became valued in their own rights, and its response to those conditions were

no longer the sole or even principal element in its success and appeal. As we have seen, no matter how much criticism the 18th-century town house received in the public sphere, people liked it for what it was, and designers began to respond to its peculiar characteristics and bring it to a peak of perfection in the later 18th and early 19th centuries. Despite the changes wrought thereafter, the truly 'classic' English town house – the Georgian terraced house – became iconic, and synonymous with classy, sleek, superior living and good taste.

ABOVE: The use of stucco characterizes John Nash's developments at Regent's Park, London (including Chester Terrace, above). Many cities have at least a patch of 'stucconia', but none as much as the capital itself.

GREAT BRITAIN

LONDON

1. Somerset House
2. Covent Garden
3. Queen Anne's Gate
4. Laurence Poutney Hill
5. Lindsey House
6. Pont Street
7. Bedford Square
8. Green Street
9. Bedford Row
10. Old Palace Yard
11. Handel House, Brook Street
12. Old Burlington Street
13. Belgrave Square
14. St James Square
15. Adam Street
16. Mecklenburgh Square
17. Gloucester Gate
18. Chester Terrace
19. Milner Square
20. Lonsdale Square
21. South Audley Street
22. Queens Gate
23. Cadogan Square
24. Cheyne Walk
25. Harley Street
26. Albert Hall Mansions
27. Wells Rise
28. The Red House, Tite Street
29. Stafford Terrace
30. Coutts Crescent, Hampstead
31. Willow Road, Hampstead

Contact Details

The houses listed below are open to the public. Please check the website, or telephone ahead for information on opening hours and admission fees.

Fairfax House
Castlegate,
York YO1 9RN
Tel: 01904 655543
www.fairfaxhouse.co.uk

Georgian House Museum
7 Great George Street
Bristol BS1 5RR
Tel: 0117 921 1362
Email: general_museum@bristol-city.gov.uk

Handel House Museum
25 Brooke Street
London W1K 4HB
Tel: 020 7495 1685
www.handelhouse.org

Linley Sambourne House
18 Stafford Terrace
London W8
www.rbkc.gov.uk/linleysambournehouse

No 1 Museum
No 1 Royal Crescent,
Bath BA1 2LR
Tel: 01225 428126
www.bath-preservation-trust.org.uk

Pickford's House Museum
41 Friar Gate
Derby DE1 1DA
Tel: 01322 255363

The Regency Town House
13 Brunswick Square,
Hove, East Sussex
BN3 IEH
www.rth.org.uk

Bibliography and Further Reading

Barron, Caroline, *Centres of Conspicuous Consumption: The Aristocratic Town House in London 1200-1500*, London Journal, 1995

Borsey, Peter, *The English Urban Renaissance: Culture and Society in the Provincial Town 1660-1770*, Oxford: Clarendon, 1989

Cruickshank, Dan and Burton, Neil, *Life in the Georgian City*, London: Viking, 1990

Cruickshank, Dan and Wyld, Peter, *London: The Art of Georgian Building*, London: Architectural Press, 1975

Girouard, Mark, *Cities and People: A Social and Architectural History*, New Haven and London: Yale University Press, 1985

Girouard, Mark, *The English Town: A History of Urban Life*, New Haven and London: Yale University Press, 1990

Jones, Edward and Woodward, Christopher. *A Guide to the Architecture of London*, London: Weidenfeld & Nicolson, 1992

Long, Helen, *The Edwardian House: The Middle-class Home in Britain 1880-1914*, Manchester and New York: Manchester University Press, 1993

Longstaffe-Gowan, Todd. *The London Town Garden 1700-1840*, New Haven and London: Yale University Press, 2001

McKellar, Elizabeth, *The Birth of Modern London: the Development and Design of the City 1660-1729*, Manchester: Manchester University Press, 1999

Mowl, Tim, *Elizabethan and Jacobean Style*, Phaidon, 1993

Mowl, Tim and Earnshaw, Brian, *Architecture Without Kings*, Manchester and New York: Manchester University Press, 1995

Muthesius, Hermann, *The English House* (1908-11), Crosby, Lockwood & Staples, 1979

Muthesius, Stefan, *The English Terraced House*, New Haven and London: Yale University Press, 1982

Parissien, Steven, *The Georgian Group Book of the Georgian House*, Aurum Press, 1995

Pevsner, Nikolaus et al, The *Buildings of England* series, New Haven and London: Yale University Press

Porter, Stephen, *The Great Fire of London*, Stroud: Sutton, 1996

Quiney, Anthony, *Town Houses of Medieval Britain*, New Haven and London: Yale University Press, 2003

Schofield, John, *Medieval London Houses*, New Haven and London: Yale University Press, 1994

Service, Alastair, *Edwardian Architecture: A Handbook to Building Design in Britain, 1890-1914*, Thames and Hudson, 1977

Service, Alastair, *London 1900*, Crosby, Lockwood & Staples, 1979

Stamp, Gavin and Amery, Colin, *Victorian Buildings of London 1837-1887: An Illustrated Guide*, London: Architectural Press, 1980

Stillman, Damie, *English Neo-classical Architecture*, vol. I, Zwemmer, 1988

Summerson, John, *Architecture in Britain 1530-1830*, 9th ed, New Haven and London: Yale University Press, 1993

Summerson, John, *Georgian London*, 3rd ed, Harmondsworth: Penguin, 1978

Summerson, John, *The Architecture of Victorian London*, Charlottesville: University Press of Virginia, 1976

Index

Author Acknowledgements

I would like to thank Ray Carlier of Croudace Homes and Richard Donnell of Savills for taking the time to explain current market and regulatory issues to me. I am also grateful for friendly and helpful responses from Bewley Homes plc, C. G. Fry & Son, and Croudace Homes. Cameron Mackintosh kindly allowed Stephen Whitehorne access to photograph their private offices, and Adrian Smith kindly allowed photography of 1 Bedford Square; the houses listed in the contact details (see page 157) also generously gave permission for photography. I am especially grateful to Steven Parissien for his help, encouragement and advice during the writing of this book. Finally, this book is dedicated to Coral and Georgia.

Picture Acknowledgements

All photography by Stephen Whitehorne, with the exception of the images listed below:

© Andrew Midgely: p.20
© Duncan Soar: p.37, 39, 130, 131, 132, 139, 140, 151
akg-images: p.36
Bewley Homes/Cadugan Place: p.143, 144
Bridgeman Art Library: p.76
C.G. Fry & Son/Poundbury, Dorchester: p.146, 147 (r,l)
Croudace Homes/Sherfield Park: p.141, 145 (r,l)
Mary Evans Picture Library: p.92
Museum of London: p. 21, p.26, 43, 119
RIBA British Architectural Library Drawings & Archives Collections: p.23
Sir John Soane's Museum: p.16, 48, 62, 64, 68, 70, 142
Suffolk Record Office: p.30
The National Trust Photo Library: p.138
V&A Images/Victoria and Albert Museum: p.24